HISTORY OF
THE ANCIENT AND MEDIEVAL WORLD

SECOND EDITION

VOLUME 6

THE EARLY MIDDLE AGES IN WESTERN ASIA AND EUROPE

Marshall Cavendish
Reference
New York

Marshall Cavendish
99 White Plains Road
Tarrytown, New York 10591

www.marshallcavendish.us

Library of Congress Cataloging-in-Publication Data

History of the ancient and medieval world / [edited by Henk Dijkstra]. --
2nd ed.
   v. cm.
 Includes bibliographical references and index.
 Contents: v. 1. The first civilizations -- v. 2. Western Asia and the
Mediterranean -- v. 3. Ancient Greece -- v. 4. The Roman Empire -- v. 5. The
changing shape of Europe -- v. 6. The early Middle Ages in western Asia and
Europe -- v. 7. Southern and eastern Asia -- v. 8. Europe in the Middle Ages
-- v. 9. Western Asia, northern Europe, and Africa in the Middle Ages -- v.
10. The passing of the medieval world -- v. 11. Index.
 ISBN 978-0-7614-7789-1 (set) -- ISBN 978-0-7614-7791-4 (v. 1) -- ISBN
978-0-7614-7792-1 (v. 2) -- ISBN 978-0-7614-7793-8 (v. 3) -- ISBN
978-0-7614-7794-5 (v. 4) -- ISBN 978-0-7614-7795-2 (v. 5) -- ISBN
978-0-7614-7796-9 (v. 6) -- ISBN 978-0-7614-7797-6 (v. 7) -- ISBN
978-0-7614-7798-3 (v. 8) -- ISBN 978-0-7614-7799-0 (v. 9) -- ISBN
978-0-7614-7800-3 (v. 10) -- ISBN 978-0-7614-7801-0 (v. 11)
1. History, Ancient. 2. Middle Ages. 3. Civilization, Medieval. I.
Dijkstra, Henk.
 D117.H57 2009
 940.1--dc22

                              2008060052

Printed in Malaysia

12 11 10 09 08 7 6 5 4 3 2 1

General Editor: Henk Dijkstra

Marshall Cavendish
Project Editor: Brian Kinsey
Publisher: Paul Bernabeo
Production Manager: Michael Esposito

Brown Reference Group
Project Editor: Chris King
Text Editors: Shona Grimbly, Charles Phillips
Designer: Lynne Lennon
Cartographers: Joan Curtis, Darren Awuah
Picture Researcher: Laila Torsun
Indexer: Christine Michaud
Managing Editor: Tim Cooke

PICTURE CREDITS

SET CONTENTS

VOLUME CONTENTS

THE NEW PERSIAN EMPIRE

The Sassanid Empire, which evolved in the early third century CE, proved to be a powerful rival to that of Rome. Among its greatest rulers were Shapur I, who defeated and captured the Roman emperor Valerian, and Khosrow I.

In the third century CE, Sassanid rulers from Persis (modern Fars) in southwestern Iran rose up against their Parthian overlords and established a great empire. At the time when the Sassanids revolted, Persis was a province within the Parthian Empire (see box, page 728). However, it had once been the center of the great Persian Empire created by the Achaemenid dynasty between the sixth and fourth centuries BCE. The new empire of the Sassanids was every bit as proud and powerful as the empire of the Achaemenids. It developed into the second great Persian Empire.

The first notable king of the Sassanid dynasty was Ardashir I. He emerged as military governor of the town of Darabgerd (close to modern Darab in Iran) and won control of several nearby cities. His father, Babak, seized the throne of Persis and was a vassal king under the Parthian ruler Artabanus V. When Babak died, Ardashir took the throne for himself, killing his own brother, Shapur, in the course of a lengthy battle against several opposing vassals of Artabanus. Ardashir was crowned king of Persis in 208 CE and proceeded to enlarge his kingdom, seizing lands on the coast of the Persian Gulf. Finally, he moved against Artabanus himself. In the Battle of Hormuz in 224 CE, Ardashir defeated the Parthians and killed Artabanus.

The king of kings

Ardashir declared himself shahanshah (king of kings)—the resonant title claimed by the kings of the Achaemenid dynasty, from the time of Darius the Great (522–486 BCE) onward—and set out to restore Persis to the glorious position it had enjoyed under the great Persian kings. He even claimed direct descent from Darius. Ardashir named his own dynasty after his grandfather Sassanid. Sassanid had been a priest of Ahura Mazda, the great god of the venerable Persian religion Zoroastrianism, which had been followed by the Achaemenid kings. Ardashir declared Zoroastrianism the national religion of his new empire. In so doing, he both honored his grandfather and strengthened his regime's links to the glorious Achaemenid Empire.

Ardashir established his capital at Ctesiphon, the Mesopotamian city once known as Babylon, which had also been the capital of the defeated Parthians. Ardashir conquered lands near and far, including Armenia, and even invaded the Punjab region of India, exacting tribute from its rulers. At home, he was celebrated for building bridges and canals and for

Ardashir I, depicted here on a gold dinar, was the first king of the Sassanid dynasty. He created a huge empire.

726

PERSIS AND THE RISE AND FALL OF PARTHIA

Persis, an ancient land in what is now south-western Iran, took its name from the tribe of the Parsua (or Persians) who made it their home in the seventh century BCE. The Parsua were one of several groups of Aryan nomads who entered the Iranian plateau from the steppes of Asia at the beginning of the first millennium BCE. The first great Persian Empire flourished between around 550 BCE and 330 BCE under the rule of the Achaemenid dynasty.

Parthia was nothing more than a satrapy or province in the Achaemenid Empire. It was eventually established as an independent kingdom around 240 BCE by the Parni, another nomadic group who were originally from the steppes between the Caspian and Aral seas. However, by the first century BCE, Parthia was the center of an empire that extended from the Euphrates River in Mesopotamia as far east as the Indus River, and from the Amu Darya River in the north as far south as the Indian Ocean. Parthia proved itself a worthy rival to the Roman Empire, and for three centuries, it held the might of Rome at bay. In 53 BCE, the Parthians won a resounding victory over the Roman general Crassus and his army at Carrhae near the Tigris River.

At the heart of the Parthian army lay its magnificent cavalry. There were two basic types of mounted soldier. The cataphracts were heavily armored—often, both the horse and its rider were protected—and were used as shock troops. The cataphract's main weapon was his lance, and charges from massed ranks of cataphracts could inflict enormous damage on the enemy. The Parthians also employed lightly armored horse archers, who often shot arrows over their shoulders as they pretended to flee, an effective practice that went down in history as "the Parthian shot."

In the second century CE, the Parthians suffered major defeats, first at the hands of the Roman emperor Trajan and then at those of Lucius Verus, co-emperor with Marcus Aurelius. By the third century CE, when the Sassanid rulers arose to launch a challenge, Parthian authority had been severely weakened.

This relief from the first century CE depicts a Parthian archer.

This stone relief from Iran depicts the emperor Shapur I.

constructing several cities, including Ardashir-Khwarrah (Glory of Ardashir) at Gur (modern Firuzabad).

Shapur's heroic exploits

At his death in 241 CE, Ardashir left a consolidated empire to his son Shapur, who proceeded to expand Sassanid power as far as the Himalayas. Shapur then undertook to fulfill a promise made to his father to conquer the Romans. He seized territory in Mesopotamia, Syria, and western Asia. In 256 CE, he sacked Antioch but was driven back by the emperor Valerian. Then, in 260 CE, Shapur defeated and captured Valerian at Edessa (modern Urfa in Turkey). Shapur gathered vast booty and huge numbers of prisoners and kept Valerian in captivity for the rest of his life. The prisoners were made to build the city of Gondeshapur (in the modern province of Khuzestan, western Iran), which was later renowned as a center of intellectual life. It was home to a university, teaching hospital, and great library. The prisoners also built a dam across the Karun River near Shushtar, afterward known as Band-i-Kaisar (Dam of Caesar).

The moment of Persia's triumph over Rome, when Shapur captured Valerian, was celebrated in a series of rock carvings. According to some accounts, Shapur humiliated Valerian by making him kneel to serve as a footstool and, after Valerian's death, had his body stuffed so that he could carry on using it in this way. A kneeling figure is depicted in the carvings, but contrary to some earlier beliefs, present-day scholars believe that it does not represent Valerian. Other accounts suggest that Shapur took the former emperor back to Persia and allowed him to live in relative comfort at Bishapur, another city built by prisoners of war.

This cameo from the fourth century CE depicts the Persian emperor Shapur I (right) in combat against the Roman emperor Valerian.

Revival of Zoroastrianism

The founders of the Sassanid Empire, Ardashir and Shapur, are celebrated for their role in establishing an agreed body of doctrine for the ancient Zoroastrian faith and collecting a number of its sacred texts. Ardashir and his priest Tosar were responsible for the treatises *The Testament of Ardashir* and *The Letter of Tosar*. Shapur played an important part in reworking the Avesta, the Zoroastrian sacred books, in particular adding fragments from ancient Greek papers on medicine, astronomy, and metaphysics to the work.

Other religions existed alongside Zoroastrianism in the Sassanid Empire. Christianity had established itself in the region under the Parthians and was strengthened by the arrival of thousands of Christians among Shapur's prisoners of war. In the eastern provinces of the empire, Buddhism was widespread as a result of large-scale missionary activity. Jews, who had lived in Babylon since their exile under Nebuchadnezzar, began to move eastward, establishing communities along the great trade and caravan routes of Mesopotamia via Iran to Afghanistan and central Asia.

During Shapur's reign, a new religion was founded by a Persian aristocrat, Mani, from southern Babylonia. Mani (c. 216–276 CE) appeared to have been influenced by Jewish sects, Christians, and Buddhist thought, as well as Greco-Roman ideas (known as Gnosticism by modern scholars) that placed great emphasis on secret knowledge revealed in visions. According to tradition, when he was 12 years old and again when he was 24, Mani had visions of an angel, "the Twin." On the second occasion, he was called to promulgate a new religion.

He traveled to India, where he made converts to his faith. On his return to the Sassanid Empire, Mani convinced the emperor to allow him to preach the new religion.

Mani considered himself the final prophet in a series that included Zoroaster, the Buddha, and Jesus. Mani's religion, Manichaeism, proposed a dualistic worldview: two principles were in competition in the world, goodness (embodied by God, light, and the soul) and evil (represented by the devil, darkness, and the body). Mani condemned the existing world as sinful and doomed, and he divided human society into two classes, the elect and the auditors (or hearers). The elect were ascetic, celibate vegetarians who would do no work other than spreading the faith; the

This modern illustration, based on an Indian fresco, depicts the prophet Mani. The religion of Manichaeism was based on his teachings.

ZOROASTER AND THE AVESTA

The sacred book of Zoroastrianism, the Avesta or Zend-Avesta, contains prayers, hymns, creation narratives, and laws. The version that survives today was assembled by Shapur I and his successors between the third and seventh centuries CE. Zoroastrians say that a much longer version existed in antiquity but was destroyed during the conquest of Persia by Alexander the Great in the fourth century BCE.

The most precious part of the Avesta is the Gathas, a collection of 17 songs or hymns believed to have been composed by the founder of Zoroastrianism himself. Zoroaster (or Zarathustra) may have lived among the Persians in the mid-sixth century BCE. According to one Zoroastrian tradition, the founder lived 258 years before Alexander the Great's

conquest of Persia, which would mean he lived around 550 BCE. However, the archaic language of the Gathas is similar to that of the Hindu scriptures of the Rig Veda (written from around 1700 BCE onward), and some scholars argue that Zoroaster in fact lived between around 1700 and 1500 BCE. Zoroastrianism and Hinduism are partially derived from a common religious and mythological framework; the separate groups of Aryan nomads who settled in India and Iran had a common origin on the steppes of Asia.

The Avesta came under threat during the Muslim invasion of Persia in the seventh century CE. Many Zorastrians fled to India, taking their scripture with them. Their modern descendants are called Parsees, and their religion in India is known as Parseeism.

THE BOOK OF KINGS

The lives of the great kings of the Achaemenid and Sassanian dynasties are described in one of the great epics of Persian literature, the *Shah-nameh* (Book of Kings), written around 1010 CE by the Muslim epic poet Firdawsi. The son of a prosperous farmer, the poet was born near Tus at the border of Turkestan. His father's wealth opened the door to a good education for Firdawsi, who learned several eastern languages. As a result, he was able to read ancient Persian historical texts, which he used as a basis for the *Shah-nameh*. He wrote the work, an epic of 60,000 verses, for Sultan Mahmud of Ghazna (a minor country in eastern Afghanistan) after Mahmud offered the poet a piece of gold for every distich (paired lines of verse) Firdawsi composed.

The *Shah-nameh* bears comparison with the *Iliad* and the *Odyssey*, the great epic poems of the ancient Greek poet Homer. Whereas the events described by Homer take place within a single generation, the *Shah-nameh* covers the entire history of Persia up to the Arab conquest in 641 CE. It even begins with a mythological account of the world's creation. The deeds of the Persian kings are fantastic: they fight with armies of elephants and horses and defeat terrifying enemies. Having spent the greater part of his working life on the epic,

Firdawsi died lonely and embittered in Tus at the age of 80, after sending his vast financial reward back to its source. He was devastated that Mahmud had betrayed him, sending the agreed number of coins in silver rather than gold.

This 17th-century-CE manuscript illustration depicts a scene from the Shah-nameh.

auditors were a larger group, permitted to marry and expected to serve the members of the elect and support them with financial gifts. At death, a member of the elect would travel to the realm of light, but an auditor would be reborn in the world. Living a good life as a member of the auditors opened the way to rebirth as a member of the elect and thus ultimately to absorption into the realm of light.

Protected by Shapur I, Mani preached all over the Sassanid Empire and sent missionaries farther afield into the Roman Empire, provoking a backlash from Zoroastrians and Christians alike. Under Shapur's successor, Bahram I (ruled 274–277 CE), Mani was arrested as a heretic. He either died in prison or was killed. His religion continued to be fiercely persecuted by Persian and Roman emperors. However, a century later, it had spread across both empires, northern Africa, and, via the Silk Route, to China.

The Sassanid golden era

The successors of Shapur I made little impact until his namesake Shapur II (ruled 309–379 CE) inaugurated a golden era. This king actually came to the throne before he was born; the crown was placed on the belly of his mother, one of the wives of the deceased King Hormizd II, while her baby was still in the womb. During his infancy and youth, Shapur II's empire was ruled by his mother and leading nobles, but after a regency of 16 years, he took power in 325 CE. He won important military victories over the Arabs, who had been raiding the southern part of the empire, and against other nomadic raiders on the empire's eastern border. Shapur conquered what is now Afghanistan and

brought it into the empire. He also won significant victories over the Romans; in 363 CE, Shapur repelled an invasion led by Emperor Julian, and Julian was killed in the battle. When Shapur died in 379 CE, the empire was at the height of its power.

The religious policy of Shapur II and his immediate successors was generally harsh. These kings were mostly tolerant of Jews but enthusiastically persecuted Christians, and this policy brought them into conflict with the Roman Empire, which had become Christian under Emperor Constantine I. However, the

This fourth-century-CE bust depicts the Sassanid emperor Shapur II.

HUNTING AND CHIVALRY: LIFE AT THE PERSIAN COURT

Persian sagas portray ideals of physical strength and skill reminiscent of western tales of chivalry. Hunting was the great sport of the Persians. Princesses and the daughters of noblemen considered it a great honor to accompany the hunters on their forays into the area between the Tigris and Euphrates rivers, which was teeming with wild animals. Craftsmen carved beautiful reliefs of worked silver that depicted these heroic hunts, showing noblemen driving game toward the king to be shot. Despite their passion for the rough pleasures of hunting, the Persians were known for their propriety and refined manners. Even among the beautiful buildings of Constantinople, the capital of the Byzantine Empire, the Persians were renowned for their refinement.

This dish, made around 550 CE, contains a portrait of Khosrow I in its center.

Sassanid emperor Yazdegerd I (ruled 399–421 CE) introduced a policy of tolerance to Christians and made peace with Rome. By this stage, the western Roman Empire was in disarray, and Sassanid dealings were with the eastern or Byzantine Empire, which was based at Constantinople or Byzantium (modern Istanbul, Turkey).

Yazdegerd's successor, Bahram V (ruled 421–438 CE) presided over another golden era for the Sassanid dynasty. He fought against Rome and in 422 CE agreed to a treaty allowing for joint religious toleration between Zoroastrians and Christians. He is lavishly celebrated in Persian folklore for the magnificence of his court (at which great music and literature were composed) and for his exploits while hunting.

Religious struggles

The importance of Christianity steadily increased in the Persian Empire during the fifth century CE. Most Christians were followers of the Nestorian Church, founded by Syrian prelate Nestorius, who served as the patriarch of Constantinople from 428 to 431 CE. He taught that humanity and divinity existed in Christ as distinct natures, not unified in a single personality. His doctrine was declared a heresy in 431 CE and he was banished. However, during the next 50 years, Nestorianism gained wide acceptance, and it was declared the official doctrine of Persian Christianity in 483 CE.

Another group of Asian nomads entered the fray in the late fifth century CE. The Hephthalites from the Mongolian steppes defeated the Persian king Firuz II in 483 CE and afterward helped another Persian king, Kavadh I (ruled 488–531 CE), regain his throne after being deposed by his brother Zamasp. The Hephthalites went on to create an empire to the east, and Kavadh battled Rome for two decades.

The rise of Khosrow I

Kavadh was finally succeeded by his son, Khosrow I, who proved to be the greatest of all Sassanid kings. He defeated the

Byzantine emperor Justinian I in a series of wars between 531 and 576 CE. Khosrow also outfought the Hephthalites, extending Persian authority west to the Black Sea, east to the Indus River, and into central Asia. He created a professional army and ordered unmarried people to wed so that they could create a new generation of recruits for it. He modernized the empire's government and tax systems, supported poor orphans out of imperial treasury funds, and built dykes and canals to supply dry cities with drinking water. He made Zoroastrianism the state religion once more and attracted philosophers from India and Greece to his palace. His reign saw another flowering of Persian literature. He was celebrated as the equal of the Achaemenid king Cyrus the Great and acclaimed as Anushirvan (Man with an Immortal Soul).

The final flourish of the Sassanids

Khosrow I's grandson Khosrow II, who ruled between 590 and 628 CE, presided over the last great era of the Sassanid dynasty. After the murder of its emperor, Mauricius, in 602 CE, Khosrow II led a great assault on the Byzantine Empire, taking Antioch in 611 CE and Damascus in 613 CE. In the following year, he captured Jerusalem and carried the holiest of Christian objects, the reliquary of Christ's cross, back to his capital, Ctesiphon. Khosrow pressed on with his campaigns and by 619 CE had conquered almost all of southwestern Asia, including Palestine and Egypt.

However, a new Byzantine emperor, Heraclius, led a devastating counterattack. Marching into Armenia and Azerbaijan and catching Khosrow II off guard in Ctesiphon, Heraclius retook the reliquary of the cross. Panic struck at the heart of the Sassanian stronghold, and Khosrow was deposed and murdered by his nobles.

Heraclius's attack effectively marked the end of the Sassanids. In just the 23 years between 628 and 651 CE, there were seven further rulers of the dynasty. None achieved greatness, and in the reign of the last Sassanid king, Yazdegerd III (ruled 632–651 CE), warlike Bedouin tribesmen from Arabia conquered the empire and imposed their new religion, Islam, on the empire's people.

This contemporary relief depicts the Persian emperor Khosrow II taking part in a deer hunt.

See also:

Mohammed and Islam (volume 6, page 736) • The Persians (volume 2, page 232) • The Rise of Islam (volume 6, page 752)

MOHAMMED AND ISLAM

The religion of Islam is based around the teachings of the prophet Mohammed, who lived in the late fifth and early sixth centuries CE. In order to establish his religion, Mohammed had to go to battle against the inhabitants of his own birthplace of Mecca.

The prophet Mohammed, founder of the religion of Islam, was born around 570 CE in the city of Mecca, Arabia. He came from an important family, one that held a key position in the administration of the Kaaba, a major shrine in Mecca at which his contemporaries worshipped a host of tribal gods.

The area of Arabia in which Mohammed grew up, which contained Mecca and the partly Jewish city of Yathrib (later Mohammed's home and called Medina), was suited to the development of new ways of thinking. With a population of traders and pilgrims, including Christians as well as a good number of Jews, the society of this area differed radically from that in the expanses of desert and isolated oases elsewhere in Arabia. Mohammed rejected the idolatry that was practiced by the Bedouin and other desert contemporaries and established a new monotheistic religion, worshipping one universal God (Allah). This religion recognized key figures of the Jewish and Christian religions, such as Abraham, Moses, and Jesus, as prophets.

The Arabian Peninsula

Throughout the Roman and Byzantine periods, and until the beginning of the seventh century CE, the Arabian Peninsula remained on the periphery of political, urban, and religious developments in the eastern part of the Mediterranean region. There were exceptions to this rule. The Nabatean kingdom, with its capital at Petra in modern Jordan, built up a great deal of wealth through trade and was annexed by the Roman emperor Trajan in the second century CE. Generally, however, the peninsula, mostly desert, attracted little attention from the imperial powers.

Most of the population of the peninsula were nomads, who relied on a pastoral economy. Although there were urban communities at the western edge of the peninsula, the largest of these cities—such as Mecca and Yathrib— were far smaller than the imperial seat of Constantinople (modern Istanbul, Turkey) and cities such as Damascus (now the capital of Syria).

The nomadic tribes inhabiting the interior of the peninsula were known as the Bedouin, from the Arabic *badawi* (plural *badu*), meaning "desert dwellers" (see box, page 738). They had to endure unforgiving heat, a barren landscape, and scarcity of water as they moved from one oasis to another with their herds. In a desert landscape without political bor-

The prophet Mohammed ascends to heaven in this 16th-century-CE illustration. The angel Gabriel hovers before him.

The inhospitable Arabian Desert has been home to the Bedouin people for thousands of years.

ders, authority covered not regions but people: the nomads owned no land; families and tribes, rather than settlements, commanded their loyalty. The only leader they recognized was the tribal elder they called sheikh. Sometimes a sheikh was chosen; sometimes he came from a prominent family. His task was not to rule directly over the tribe (the individualistic desert dwellers would not have tolerated that); it was to find workable solutions to the conflicts endemic among the groups of desert nomads. All too often, small problems would escalate into deadly feuds involving large numbers of people. When entire tribes were drawn into the cycle of violence, the result could be wars lasting for years.

The caravan city of Mecca grew around the Kaaba (cube), a temple that

THE BEDOUIN NOMADS

A nomadic desert people of the Middle East, the Bedouin traditionally lived in the deserts of what are now Iraq, Syria, and Jordan as well as Arabia. Their lifestyle altered little for hundreds of years, but in the 20th century CE, especially after World War II (1939–1945 CE), many Bedouin began to live as settled farmers in cities.

Traditional Bedouins were herders of camels, goats, and sheep who moved from oasis to oasis, seeking out the sparse meadows found nearby. They subsisted on the milk of their camels, occasional meat from their herds of sheep and goats, and figs and dates from the oasis palms. They traded for rice, other food items, and the few essentials they used.

The Bedouin nomads were fierce fighters, and bloody feuds ran between different groups. Deeds of war were celebrated. Each tribe had its own poet, who recorded the exploits of its warriors in verse. Tribal wars were the basis of epic poems. Mohammed had a Bedouin wet nurse, and he lived among the desert nomads for much of his early childhood. The Bedouin lifestyle had a great influence on him.

housed figurines representing the various gods worshipped by the tribes of the Arabian Peninsula. Pilgrims flocked to the Kaaba, and the city teemed with traders. Mecca had something of a cosmopolitan atmosphere; there was a Jewish neighborhood, and the city's residents also included a few Christians and many traders from the Mediterranean. As well as being a trading post and religious site, it was known as a popular center for poetry festivals.

Historical sources

The principal sources for the life of Mohammed are religious documents: the Koran, early biographies, and the hadith. The hadith were oral biographical traditions that were later written down by the prophet's followers. Muslims believe the Koran to be the words of God as dictated to a scribe by Mohammed in his lifetime, but most historians agree that the Koran was written down by Mohammed's companions either before or shortly after his death in 632 CE. The oldest known biographies of Mohammed are ninth-century-CE versions by Ibn Hisham and Al-Waqidi of a now-lost document called *Sirat Rasul Allah* (The Life of God's Prophet). The original was reputedly written in the eighth century CE by the historian Ibn Ishaq. The hadith were passed down orally for more than a century after Mohammed's death and first written down in the early to mid-eighth century CE.

Some seventh-century-CE documents by Christian and Jewish groups also make reference to Mohammed. Written in Greek, Hebrew, Armenian, and Syriac, they mention that he was a merchant and preacher and that his teachings centered on the figure of Abraham. The documents also refer to Mohammed's escape from Mecca to Medina.

According to Islamic tradition, Mohammed's father, Abd-Allah, died

A young Bedouin poses with a camel. The nomadic Bedouin people have herded camels for thousands of years.

three months before the birth of his son in 570 CE. The infant was given to a Bedouin wet nurse, who cared for him in the desert for two years. As an adult, Mohammed would remember only this nurse from his earliest years. When the wet nurse returned the child at the end of the two years, his mother asked her to take him away once more, saying: "Take the child with you again, and return to the desert, so that he does not become ill from the unhealthy air of Mecca."

Mohammed spent another three years in the tents of the Bedouin, becoming familiar at a very young age with their traditions and ways of thinking. "I am an Arab from head to toe," he would later say, "I come from the Quaraish of Mecca, and speak the language of the Beni Assas [the Bedouin tribe of his wet nurse]."

When he was five years old, Mohammed returned to the house of his mother in Mecca. However, she died eight months later and he was sent to live with his grandfather. Three years after that, his grandfather also died. Now nine years old, Mohammed was sent to the home of his uncle Abu Talib. Perhaps because of Mohammed's early bereavements, care for people without parents later became a key requirement of the Islamic faith.

Marriage to Khadijah

Mohammed's family was not rich. His father left him three camels and a slave. His uncle owned a small flock of goats and sheep that Mohammed tended on the dry plains around Mecca. "There has never been a prophet who has not been a shepherd," he would later say. Abu Talib was not just a farmer. Like most residents of Mecca, he was also active in trade. The merchants pooled their resources to send caravans across the desert to Damascus in Syria and to Egypt. When Abu Talib could no longer support his nephew, he

The city of Mecca. All Muslims are expected to make at least one pilgrimage to Mecca.

advised him to find a job with the caravans sent out by the rich widow Khadijah. Mohammed entered her employment. Although she was 15 years his senior, they married that same year, in 595 CE. However, the marriage was not made for financial reasons; years later, Mohammed would tell his friends that he had never loved anyone more than he loved Khadijah.

At the age of 25, Mohammed had a wife, money, and a successful business. He could have dedicated himself to the pleasant life of a stay-at-home merchant. His caravans trekked through Arabia, bringing him and his wife new riches. However, Mohammed rejected this life to devote himself to religion.

Religious visions

As a young child with the Bedouin, Mohammed had experienced the loneliness of the desert; he knew the sacred traditions of the desert peoples and was familiar with the religious beliefs celebrated at the Kaaba shrine in Mecca. According to tradition, Mohammed habitually went on retreat to a cave in Mount Hira near Mecca. Around his 40th year (610 CE), he began to experience visions. One of them involved an encounter with the angel Gabriel, where Mohammed was told that he was the Messenger of God.

Returning home, Mohammed was badly shaken and told Khadijah of his experience. She was supportive of him and took him to her cousin Waraqah ibn Nawfal, a Christian convert, who also encouraged Mohammed. Visions and revelations were not considered unusual in Arabia, especially in Meccan society, where people were readily open to religious experience. In Mohammed's own time, one familiar sight was an epileptic Jewish youth from Medina who walked around softly humming prophecies through his teeth. This type of humming

was the standard form of prophesying. Arabian *kahins* (priests or guardians of the shrines) regularly went into trances; the sound they brought forth was called *sach* (meaning "the cooing of doves").

Nevertheless, Mohammed experienced continued difficulties; he wanted to be sure that his visions really came from God. If a jinn or evil spirit had taken possession of him—and such things were considered to be possible at any time—then he would not have become a true prophet. Mohammed then prayed and underwent spiritual disciplines, and the revelations returned. On some occasions, an angel appeared. On others, the holy

This Turkish miniature from either the late 16th or early 17th century CE depicts the prophet Mohammed (top left) with his cousin Ali.

741

THE KAABA

Muslims see the Kaaba shrine in the Great Mosque in Mecca as the holiest place on earth. They bow toward it during their prayers five times each day and are expected to visit it on pilgrimage at least once during their lifetime. Made of marble and gray stone, it is shaped like a cube—its name means "cube" in Arabic—and its corners are aligned with the points of the compass. Inside are three roof pillars and a number of suspended silver and gold lamps, as well as the Black Stone of Mecca, said to have been given to Adam when he was expelled from paradise.

Religious tradition also reports that the Kaaba was built by the ancient Jewish patriarch Abraham and his son Ishmael, using the foundations of an even older structure raised by Adam himself. The Kaaba was a religious shrine for Arabs in the days before Islam, when it housed more than 300 statues of idols; pilgrims came from all over the Arabian Peninsula to worship there. The Prophet cleansed it and cleared it of idols on his triumphant return to Mecca from Medina in 630 CE.

Pilgrims circle the Kaaba, the holiest shrine in the Islamic world.

message was transmitted in other ways. Mohammed complained: "Sometimes it comes to me in the sound of a clock, and the most painful thing for me is that I then lose it, and must remember what was said. At times it comes to me as a man who comes to talk to me, and then I remember his words."

The revelations were exhausting. According to tradition, when Mohammed experienced his visions, he perspired heavily, even on the coldest days. Mohammed was instructed to begin preaching, and he began to speak publicly in Mecca in 613 CE.

The religion of Mohammed

Many of Mohammed's contemporaries venerated the moon, stars, and tribal deities in the form of idols in the Kaaba, the traditional shrine in Mecca. They believed heaven and earth to be populated by innumerable gods, headed by the one they called Allah (Arabic for "God").

What Mohammed learned by revelation from the angel Gabriel was that there was just one God, and that he was creator of all that existed. Far more than a tribal god of the Arabian nomads, Allah was universal, good, and just. Mohammed considered that Yahweh of the Jews and the God of the Christians were simply other manifestations of the one God that he called Allah.

Allah, Mohammed taught, demanded honor from all mortals. He rewarded the devout and punished the wicked. Mohammed believed that when people directed prayers toward nonexistent gods, they were not only wasting their time but also insulting Allah—and for this they would be punished. Mohammed forbade idolatry, even as practiced by his own tribe, the Quaraish.

Mohammed had few followers at first. They included his wife, Khadijah, his cousin Ali, a son of Abu Talib, and the house slave Said. Mohammed's first convert outside the family was the merchant Abu Bakr. One of Mohammed's requirements was that his followers could not be slaves, so attempts had to be made to buy the freedom of any converts who were slaves. According to tradition, Abu Bakr spent 4,000 silver coins on buying the freedom of slaves. In so doing, he enhanced Mohammed's popularity among the poor and exploited. A slave named Bilal converted around this time. He was noted for the quality of his voice, and he became the first muezzin (announcer of the hour of prayer) to call the faithful to worship.

Mohammed also attracted the interest of the wealthy. Three rich merchants—Talha, Abderrahman, and Othman—converted, giving their fortunes to the

Muslims pray at a mosque in Germany in 2006. Muslims are expected to pray five times a day, facing Mecca when they do so.

JIHAD AND THE SPREAD OF ISLAM

The word *jihad* literally means "to make an effort" (implicitly, for the sake of the cause) but is popularly interpreted as meaning "holy war." The concept developed alongside Islam itself. In the early days of the religion, the jihad took several forms. These included participating in the defense of the Muslim community, donating money or goods to the community, and overcoming the temptation to return to pagan beliefs. The term became popular as a description of Muslim conquest, especially in the early periods of Islamic history.

In Islamic tradition, there are understood to be four ways of waging the holy war of jihad: in the heart, using the tongue, by hand, and with a sword. Jihad in the heart consists of fighting temptation, while jihad of the tongue and hand is a matter of doing right and avoiding wrong in speech and daily activity. Jihad of the sword is conflict undertaken to combat enemies of Islam.

Mohammed taught that his convictions should be defended with weapons. Even in Medina, battle had been an essential part of Jihad. The idea behind this physical waging of holy war was that the world was divided into two areas—one belonging to Allah, ruled on his behalf by his faithful followers, and one subject to chaos. It was the task of Allah's followers to combat and diminish chaos, both on the individual and the social levels.

In modern Islam, most commentators emphasize the inner nature of jihad—the combat within every individual against wrong action and beliefs; many justify physical violence only in cases where Islam is in danger and must be defended.

young religion. In general, however, Mohammed's forthright denunciation of traditional forms of worship and opposition to slavery made him unpopular with the established classes in Mecca. Many members of his own tribe, who sold food, water, and ritual robes around the Kaaba, lost money as the new religion won converts.

The initial indifference of many in Mecca turned to antipathy and persecution. Mohammed and his followers withdrew to the house of Abu Talib on the outskirts of Mecca. They stayed there for three years, in increasingly difficult circumstances. The town authorities stoned and beat converts when they saw them. In 619 CE, the prophet's kinsmen in the Quaraish tribe withdrew their protection. During this time, both Khadijah and Abu Talib died.

A muezzin calls the faithful to prayer. The first muezzin was a former slave named Bilal who lived at the time of Mohammed.

The hegira

Eventually, the situation became unbearable. Mohammed had a vision that told him to leave for Yathrib, 250 miles (400 km) north of Mecca. In September of 622 CE, he departed in the company of 100 disciples. The date of the flight (or hegira), September 20, would become the first day of the Islamic calendar.

Mohammed and his followers made their escape safely. Before approaching Yathrib itself, they waited a few days in Koba, an outlying town near Yathrib. Mohammed wanted to gauge what the popular reaction would be if his disciples entered the city. When all seemed quiet, they proceeded toward Yathrib. It was a Friday when they made their approach.

Just outside the gates, Mohammed climbed down from his camel to pray. A mosque was later built on the spot, and Friday became celebrated as the Islamic holy day. In time, Yathrib was renamed Madinat al-Nabi (City of the Prophet). It later became known simply as Madinah or Medina.

The city was a favorable breeding ground for Mohammed's teachings. The Jewish tribes who made up a large section of the population were committed to monotheism. According to tradition, Mohammed was welcomed by cheering crowds, who called out: "Step down, prophet, from your camel and stay with us. We have room for you, and weapons with which to protect you." Mohammed

This Mosque of Mohammed Ali stands in Cairo, Egypt. According to Islamic belief, the first mosque was built at Medina by the prophet Mohammed.

replied that he would leave the decision to his animal. The weary camel came to rest beside a courtyard, where a few palm trees grew. It is said that Mohammed stayed in this spot and built his first mosque there. From these humble beginnings, great things grew. Within just 10 years, Mohammed was political and spiritual leader of Medina, and his followers made up the majority of the city's population.

Wars with Mecca

The Meccans did not leave their runaway son in peace. They launched a series of assaults on Medina and Mohammed's followers. In 624 CE, with an army of just 300, Mohammed won a great victory over a 1,000-strong Meccan force near the marketplace of Badr. The triumph was hailed as proof of God's blessing on the new religion and its prophet. The warriors who took part in this famous battle became known as the *badriyun* and are seen by present-day Muslims as members of the Companions of Mohammed, an elite group who had personal contact with the Prophet.

The following year, however, Mohammed and his troops were defeated at Mount Uhud, around 5 miles (8 km) from Medina. The Meccan cavalry inflicted substantial losses on the Muslims, and Mohammed himself was injured. One reason for the defeat was that part of the Muslim army deserted the field of battle to look for booty. The defeat was thus also seen as divinely ordained. It was later argued that if the Muslims had not been distracted by the pursuit of earthly goods, Allah would have granted them victory. After Uhud, Medina itself was besieged. However, Mohammed outwitted the attackers by digging a wide defensive trench that the Meccans were unable to cross.

In these battles, the Jews in Medina took up an impartial position at best. Mohammed carried out stern measures against them, banning a number of their people from the city, killing others, and forcing the rest into subservient positions. After seizing Jewish possessions around the city, Mohammed devised a law that Muslims have applied for centuries to people of other religions: the Jews could continue to exercise their beliefs under official protection but had to pay a special tax to do so.

By 628 CE, Mecca was willing to sign a ten-year truce. The subsequent Treaty of al-Hudaybiyah also recognized Mohammed's political authority and gave Muslims free access to the Kaaba. In 629 CE, Mohammed led the first pilgrimage to Mecca. The pilgrimage resulted in thousands of conversions, even among the urban elite.

Mohammed leads his followers to victory in the Battle of Badr. This manuscript illustration was created in the late 16th century CE.

Return to Mecca

When, at the beginning of 630 CE, Mohammed returned to Mecca with 10,000 followers, the city offered little resistance. He rode his camel seven times around the Kaaba, ordered the idols destroyed, and rededicated the building to Allah (see box, page 742). However, Mohammed made it possible for his erstwhile enemies to work for him. He gave them honorable positions and allowed them to share in the spoils for war. His many victories had a great impact even on those who were skeptical of his religious message.

A wave of conversions occurred among the Bedouin; representatives of several tribes came to offer their spiritual and political submission to Mohammed. He became a theocrat (someone who rules through divinely bestowed, religious authority) and united the disparate feuding tribes of the desert into a brotherhood called the *ummah*. Mohammed's control was rooted in the theological conviction of his supporters.

Gradually, Mohammed began treating his opponents with less tolerance. In 631 CE, he formally announced the persecution of remaining nonbelievers. At the conclusion of the holy period (when differences were traditionally put aside), Mohammed said that nonbelievers would be declared outlaws and denied permission to worship near the Kaaba. This declaration brought him more converts. By 632 CE, few Arabs had failed to embrace the religion of Mohammed, at least outwardly.

The final years of Mohammed

Right up to the end of his life, Mohammed lived humbly and in poverty, shaking the lice from his blankets himself and saddling his own camel. Like the Bedouin nomads with whom he spent his earliest years, he lived on dates and curdled milk. He was revered as a spiritual leader, the founder of a holy state dedicated to the greater glory of Allah rather than to his own aggrandizement. Mohammed made no attempt to take financial advantage of his followers; he was satisfied with a low tax, sufficient to meet the costs of his administration. He carried out that administration in a moderate fashion, fulfilling the traditional role of a sheikh—to prevent or solve conflicts among his people. In general,

In this 18th-century-CE illustration, pilgrims arrive at the holy city of Medina.

747

his administration was extremely successful. No rebellions were reported, even after his death.

In 632 CE, Mohammed fell ill and died. The faithful spread legends concerning his death. According to one, Allah sent an angel down to ask his great servant whether he wished to remain alive. Mohammed replied that he wanted whatever God wanted, and his last words were: "God forgive me, and allow me to come to you in heaven." At the time of his death, Arabia was largely unified under his new religion.

Islam and Muslims

The creed of Islam, as formulated by Mohammed, is stated in a single phrase: "There is no god but Allah, and Mohammed is his prophet." Followers of Islam (which means "surrender," that is, to the will of Allah) are called Muslims (the Arabic word for "those who submit"). They revere Mohammed as the greatest of a line of prophets that also includes Noah, Abraham (said to be the forefather of the Arabs through his son Ishmael and of the Jews through his son Isaac), and Moses, who gave the Hebrews their laws some five centuries after Abraham first spoke to them of Yahweh. Jesus is likewise honored as a prophet, but he is regarded as human, not divine.

The religion's basic tenets, as written in the Koran, state: "We believe in God and in that which has been sent down on us and … on Abraham, Ishmael, Isaac, and Jacob, and their progeny, and that which was given to Moses and Jesus and the Prophets by their Lord; we make no distinction among any of them and to him we submit" (Sura II, 136). The Koran adds: "True piety is this: to believe in God, and the Last Day, and the angels; the Book [the Koran], and the Prophets; to give of one's substance, however cherished, to kinsmen and orphans, the needy, the traveler, beggars, and to free the slave; to perform the prayer; to pay the alms. And they who fulfill their covenant … these are the truly godfearing" (Sura II, 177).

According to Islamic tradition, Allah ordered 104 books to descend from heaven to present truth to humankind.

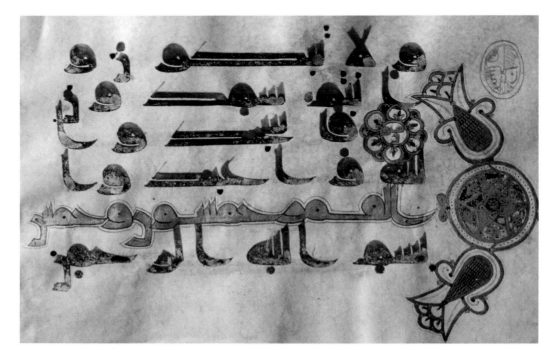

This page from the Koran was created in the ninth century CE. Muslims believe that the Koran is the word of Allah, as revealed to the prophet Mohammed.

The first man, Adam, received 10 books; other biblical figures were also given their share—Abraham had 10, Moses one. However, over the course of time, almost all of these books were lost; only the one given to Moses (now the first five books of the Bible), the psalms of David, the gospel of Jesus, and the Koran (given to Mohammed himself) survived. Of these, only the Koran is seen as entirely reliable.

Mohammed added to the Koran's verses throughout his life as new revelations came to him. These revelations were organized after his death into 114 chapters called suras. The other scriptures were, in Mohammed's view, distorted by the Jews and Christians who had lost track of pure monotheism. The greatest distortion, he said, was the claim that Jesus was the Son of God. This assault on the majesty of Allah was unthinkable for Mohammed.

The Koran establishes five obligations for the faithful. The first is acceptance of the basic creed that Allah is the only god

and that Mohammed is his prophet. The second is the obligation to pray. *Salah* (ritual prayer) is to be performed five times daily—at dawn, noon, late afternoon, sunset, and after dark. The person doing the praying is expected to face Mecca. Before the prayers, ablutions with water (or sand) are to be performed. *Du'a* (private prayer), on the other hand, can be performed at any time.

The Koran insists that belief be put into practice in the form of good deeds and the giving of alms to the poor. This duty is the third requirement. The good deeds are done to Allah, who wants to see the belief of his servants confirmed in practice. According to the hadith, Mohammed said: "A man's true wealth hereafter is the good he does in this world to his fellow men." The fourth obligation is to fast during the holy month of Ramadan, while the fifth is to make at least one hajj (pilgrimage) to Mecca during one's lifetime.

Men from the Tuareg tribe lead a camel caravan through the deserts of Algeria. Caravans such as this were used in Mohammed's day to transport goods across Arabia.

Much of the Koran employs vivid language. On the Day of Resurrection, it teaches, the dead will rise to be judged. The righteous will cross a bridge to eternal bliss in lush gardens of delight, where fountains spout wine (forbidden to mortals while they live) and tables are laden with food, beds are soft, and houris (young virgins) grant caresses to each blessed soul. Wives will respect these houris; at the right hand of God, there can be no jealousy. The damned, on the other hand, will be thrown into an abyss to wear garments of fire that torment their skin, which will grow back only to be repeatedly destroyed. Surrounded by decay, they will writhe in agony as they drink boiling liquids.

The first caliph

Mohammed had not named a successor. He was survived by his daughter Fatima and her two sons, Hassan and Hussein. Various parties of converts attempted to take power. Mohammed's former companions finally settled on Abu Bakr, the merchant who had spent so generously to free early Muslim converts among the slaves of Mecca and who had been Mohammed's traveling companion on the hegira. Abu Bakr was declared *khalifat rasul Allah* (Successor to God's Prophet) or caliph and given the authority of Mohammed himself. Like Mohammed, Abu Bakr was both spiritual and political leader of the faithful.

Abu Bakr was the first of a long succession of caliphs who ruled over Muslims for centuries. There was no separation of political and religious establishments in Muslim regions; a caliph had both political and religious obligations. The later rulers of Baghdad, Cairo, and Córdoba (all Muslim cities) preached

The prophet Mohammed (reclining) is depicted with his successor, Abu Bakr, in this 17th-century-CE miniature.

each Friday in the mosques. At one point, the caliph of Baghdad denounced his subjects for having an unworthy lifestyle. In practice, however, the spiritual element of a caliphate was often pushed into the background as individual caliphs became preoccupied with other issues of government.

Fighting for Islam

Abu Bakr himself ruled for only two years. During that time, he held off the domestic enemies of Islam, consolidating Muslim authority in central Arabia. At the northern border, his Bedouin tribesmen began to act aggressively against the two great powers of his time, Persia and the eastern Roman Empire. The victories of these Bedouin warriors in what is now Iraq and Syria were the first of many Muslim conquests.

The Bedouin, who made up the bulk of the Muslim army at this time, had never undertaken more than an occasional marauding expedition. However, in the wake of their conversion to Islam, they made an effective fighting force. The warriors' intense religious faith was crucial; they were bent on conquest for religious purposes. They believed that they had the protection of Allah. Convinced that defeat was impossible, they attacked their opponents with considerable zeal.

The concept that early Muslims had of their conquests was entirely different from the nature of previous military campaigns, such as those of Alexander the Great and the Romans. The purpose of the jihad was the establishment of a rule that the warriors believed in their hearts to be blessed by God and to be just.

See also:

The Caliphate (volume 6, page 764) • The Riches of Islam (volume 6, page 776) • The Rise of Islam (volume 6, page 752)

THE RISE OF ISLAM

From small beginnings in the early seventh century CE, Islam spread quickly over vast areas of Africa, Asia, and Europe. One hundred years later, Arab warriors had conquered Spain in the west and stood on the border of China in the east.

In the century following the death of the prophet Mohammed (in 632 CE), Bedouin warriors carried his religion of Islam as far to the northwest as Spain and as far to the east as India and China. By the middle of the eighth century CE, Islam extended over a greater area than the Roman Empire had at its height. The success of the new faith was due in part to the zeal of the conquering Islamic armies, but mainly to the weaknesses of the existing powers in western Asia and the eastern Mediterranean.

While Mohammed had been establishing Islam in Medina (620–630 CE), the Byzantine emperors and the kings of Persia had been involved in an attritional struggle. Under Khosrow II (ruled 590–628 CE), Persian soldiers advanced to the banks of the Bosporus Straits; the Byzantine emperor Heraclius had almost been able to see his enemies from his capital, Constantinople. Heraclius's forces then drove the Persian troops back into their own territory. The war was costly to both sides; by the end of it, neither Khosrow nor Heraclius had the forces to combat the unexpected onslaught of fierce Bedouin tribesmen fighting for Islam and for Abu Bakr, the religion's first caliph (successor to Mohammed).

The Islamic warriors were sent out by Abu Bakr with an uncommonly benign code of ethics. The caliph declared: "I have ten commandments to give you. Do not cheat and do not steal. Do not betray. Do not injure anyone. Kill no children, women, or old people. Burn no palm trees. Cut down no fruit trees. Do not destroy any harvests. Kill no livestock or camels, unless this shall be to obtain food for yourselves. Make offerings to the monks with shorn heads. Leave the hermits alone." For once, the civilian populations had little to fear. Unlike plundering gangs of mercenaries, Arab armies normally allowed civilians to carry on with business as usual. The ordinary people thus had little reason to resist their conquerors.

The rule of Caliph Omar

Abu Bakr ruled for just two years (632–634 CE), but before he died, he appointed a successor, Omar bin Khattab. Omar bin Khattab was a Muslim merchant who had joined Mohammed in Mecca before the flight to Medina and, like both Mohammed and Abu Bakr, was a member of the Quaraish tribe of Mecca. Omar ruled for 10 years (634–644 CE) and was a highly effective and powerful caliph. In his inaugural speech, in the mosque at Medina,

Persia (modern Iran) has been a Muslim country since the seventh century CE. These mosques are in the Iranian city of Yazd.

THE GROWTH OF THE ISLAMIC WORLD

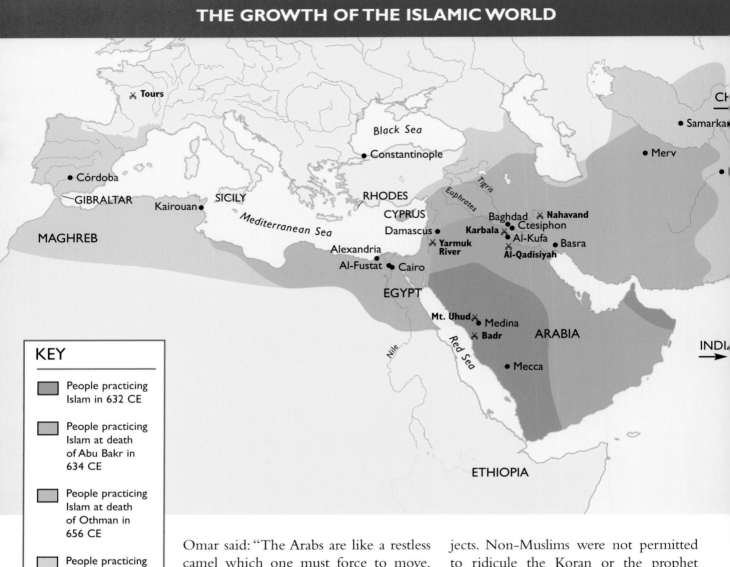

KEY

People practicing Islam in 632 CE

People practicing Islam at death of Abu Bakr in 634 CE

People practicing Islam at death of Othman in 656 CE

People practicing Islam at fall of Umayyad dynasty in 750 CE

✗ Major battle

Omar said: "The Arabs are like a restless camel which one must force to move. On the God of the Kaaba, I swear to you that I shall lead you where you must go." While his generals achieved great successes everywhere, Omar directed strategy from Medina. His plan was superbly successful. Attacking Persia and the eastern Roman (Byzantine) Empire simultaneously, the Islamic armies conquered the Byzantines in Syria and drove the Persians out of Mesopotamia. Arab troops took Damascus in 635 CE.

Caliph Omar was the first caliph to be known by the title *amir al-mu'minin* (commander of the faithful). He laid down strict rules of conduct for his new subjects. Non-Muslims were not permitted to ridicule the Koran or the prophet Mohammed, to marry Muslim women, to attempt to convert a Muslim, to wound or rob anyone, or to help the enemies of Islam. In addition, they had to be recognizable by their clothing. Non-Muslims were not permitted to build houses taller than those of Muslims; they were forbidden to read their scriptures aloud or to ring bells (the standard way of calling Christians to worship); they were not allowed to ride horses, but they were permitted to use mules or donkeys; and they could not drink wine in public and had to keep their pigs hidden from view. (Pigs are considered unclean in Islam.)

Military triumphs

In August of 636 CE, Arab forces won an important victory over the Byzantines at the Yarmuk River on the southern rim of the Golan Heights. The following year, after defeating the Persian army in the Battle of al-Qadisiyah, they captured the Persian capital, Ctesiphon; Yazdegerd III, the last Sassanid king of Persia, fled the city. The Arabs triumphed again at the Battle of Nahavand in 642 CE, and by 643 CE, they had taken control of Persia. Yazdegerd was alive but on the run; he was killed in 651 CE at Merv, and with his death, the Sassanid era ended. Around the same time, Arab armies moved into Egypt and forced the Byzantines out of Alexandria.

The Arabs consolidated their territorial gains by building fortified towns—Al-Fustat in Egypt, Basra and Al-Kufa in Mesopotamia. Far more than military camps, these were places where Arabian traditions and lifestyle were maintained.

The vast stores of goods seized from the conquered rulers were exploited by the new government. The income went directly to Medina, where the caliph used them to pay his veterans.

In 644 CE, Caliph Omar was assassinated by a non-Muslim Persian slave, Abu-Lu'lu'ah, who harbored a grudge against the caliph. The slave, who was a Zoroastrian, stabbed Omar six times as the caliph led morning prayers in a mosque in Medina; Omar died two days later of his wounds. As he lay dying, he discussed the choice of a successor with his advisers; in the end, the decision was left to a council of elders. They chose Othman ibn Affan, another one of Mohammed's original converts. Once appointed, Othman, a former cloth merchant and moneylender, filled key positions with old associates from Mecca's mercantile aristocracy, particularly members of his own Umayyad clan of the Quaraish tribe. Othman's policy aroused

Mesopotamia (modern Iraq) was another early Arab conquest. This is a mosque in the Iraqi city of Basra.

were heightened further by religious disputes about the text and the correct interpretation of the Koran.

The first schism

When Othman was murdered in his own house in 656 CE, the various factions abandoned all attempts at maintaining unity. Ali took over as caliph and moved his capital from Medina to Al-Kufa (the garrison town founded by Omar), where he had numerous supporters. Ali's chief opponent was Mu'awiyah, a leading member of the Ummayad clan who, in 640 CE, had been named governor of Syria by Othman. Mu'awiyah came to prominence despite the fact that his father had been one of Mohammed's greatest enemies. As governor of Syria, Mu'awiyah had won great victories against the Byzantines, including the capture of Cyprus in 649 CE and Rhodes in 654 CE. Mu'awiyah was also a kinsman of Othman, and he believed that Ali had been involved in Othman's murder; therefore, although he did not take part in the failed rebellion against Ali led by the Prophet's widow, Aisha, he refused to acknowledge Ali's authority.

The result was civil war. Ali's troops marched into Syria and clashed with Mu'awiyah's army in the Battle of Siffin on the bank of the Euphrates River in 657 CE. On the third day of the battle, Mu'awiyah appeared to have lost; his soldiers attached pages from the Koran to their spears and advanced shouting that the Book, not the sword, should decide the conflict. They wanted to resolve the matter through peaceful negotiation rather than violence. The two sides agreed to a period of arbitration, and the battle ended. Six months later, the representatives appointed to make the decision agreed to depose both Ali and Mu'awiyah and to allow the people to choose their caliph. Ali's representative made this announcement, but he was

This Turkish painting from the 16th century CE depicts the death of Hassan ben Ali, grandson of the prophet Mohammed.

hostility from other groups, who perceived it as favoritism. The opposition rallied around Mohammed's cousin and son-in-law, Ali. Ali's wife, Fatima, was the Prophet's daughter by his first wife, Khadijah. Revolution was in the air. Many Bedouin felt that a disproportionate amount of the profits from war and peace had gone to Medina. Tensions

then tricked by Mu'awiyah's spokesman, who claimed the caliphate for his candidate. Naturally, Ali did not accept the decision and continued as caliph. While Mu'awiyah did not actually claim the caliphate, he remained governor of Syria and moved to take control of Egypt. The standoff continued, but Mu'awiyah was now stronger and Ali was weaker.

Many Muslims were unhappy with this return to the status quo. Believing the conflict to be harmful to their religion, they hatched a new plot. At almost the same hour on the same Friday in 661 CE, Mu'awiyah and Ali were both stabbed with poisoned swords as they prayed in their respective mosques. Mu'awiyah was wearing armor beneath his clothing and was not mortally wounded, but Ali died two days later from his wounds.

Ali's supporters appointed Ali's son Hassan as caliph, and Hassan's supporters rallied around him. Mu'awiyah marched against them. After an inconclusive battle, Mu'awiyah sent envoys to negotiate a settlement, and Hassan agreed to abandon his claim to the caliphate, making Mu'awiyah the undisputed leader of Islam. He ruled as caliph in Damascus until his death in 680 CE.

On Mu'awiyah's death, Ali's second son, Hussein, marched to Al-Kufa to claim the caliphate. On October 10, 680 CE, the army of Mu'awiyah's son, Yazid, encountered Hussein at Karbala, around 60 miles (100 km) southwest of Baghdad, and slaughtered him, along with 70 members of his family and staff.

The murder of Hussein immortalized his cause. Ever since, large numbers of Muslims have regarded Mu'awiyah and his family as usurpers, violators of the Koran. Those who believed that the spirit of Mohammed was inherited by Ali formed the Shi'ite sect of Islam (see box, page 758). The date of the Battle of Karbala is commemorated in Islamic countries to this day, and reenactments of the massacre are performed at Karbala as part of the festival of Ashura, a day of fasting and mourning.

Civilian conversions

In spite of all the factional disputes, the power of the Arabs continued to grow. The Arabs broke the last resistance of the Persians; they forced the Byzantine army back to the mountains of Asia Minor, thwarting its attempts to recover lost land; and they brought the Syrians and the Egyptians under Islamic rule. The

This illustration from around 1600 CE depicts Yazid's victory over Hussein at the Battle of Karbala in 680 CE.

SUNNI AND SHI'ITE MUSLIMS

The split between the Sunni and Shi'ite Muslims goes back to seventh-century-CE disputes over the succession to the prophet Mohammed. Sunni Muslims believe that the first four caliphs—Abu Bakr, Omar, Othman, and Mu'awiyah—were the Prophet's rightful heirs. Shi'ite Muslims, on the other hand, believe that the leadership of Islam should have passed to Mohammed's son-in-law and cousin, Ali, and his descendants, the Alids. They reject the authority of the first four caliphs and maintain that Ali was the rightful leader by virtue of being the very first convert to Islam and the husband of Mohammed's daughter Fatima. The Shi'ites developed their own theology and legal system, emphasizing Ali's right to the caliphate as one who had been chosen rather than elected.

The Shi'ite name comes from that of Ali's original supporters, the *shi'at Ali* (party of Ali), while the Sunnis are so called because they claim to follow Mohammed's *sunna* (example). Shi'ites are in the majority in Iraq and Iran, but elsewhere, they are greatly outnumbered by Sunni Muslims; around 90 percent of the world's Muslims are Sunnis. The Shi'ites do not speak of a caliph but of an imam. The term means "leader of the community" and is used to refer to Islamic holy men. Shi'ites believe that a series of 12 imams, descended from Ali and Fatima, had the right to leadership of the Muslims. According to the Shi'ites, the last imam disappeared and will return at the end of the world. For Sunni Muslims, the caliph is an elected leader, liable to human error and sin but worthy of respect and obedience for as long as he maintains Islam. Shi'ites believe that imams are appointed or chosen by Allah himself and are given insights by him. As a result, they have absolute spiritual authority. (Imam is also an honorary title given to the trained leaders of prayer in mosques.)

A Shi'ite Muslim studies a book in Qom (Iran). The city is the world's leading center of Islamic scholarship and a place of pilgrimage.

next issue was whether or not the vanquished would accept the religion of the conquerors.

There were several practical benefits in adopting Islam. Conversion freed people from the obligation to pay head tax, and Islamic law stipulated that believers could not be slaves. Slowly but surely, the great majority of the conquered people chose Islam. Their decision was aided by the ease with which conversion could be made; the only requirement for a convert was to acknowledge that there was no god but Allah and that Mohammed was his prophet. The new Muslims adopted the language of their conquerors; Coptic and Aramaic gave way to Arabic. These conversions did not all happen overnight, and there were some refusals; there are tales of entire villages that moved to Christian Asia Minor, under the protection of Byzantine soldiery. Moreover, some groups stayed put while holding on to their existing beliefs; their descendants today are the people of the Christian Church in Syria and the Coptic Christians in Egypt and Ethiopia.

Western expansion

The Arabs were not content with the conquest of Syria and Egypt; their warriors continued westward. They encountered resistance from the Berbers of the Atlas Mountains, but after building the fortress city of Kairouan (in modern Tunisia), the Arabs proceeded to subdue the Maghreb region of northwestern Africa. Toward the end of the seventh century CE, the Arab armies reached the Atlantic Ocean. To the north, in plain view across the narrow straits at the entrance to the Mediterranean Sea, lay the Iberian Peninsula of western Europe. The land directly in the Arabs' sights was Hispania (present-day Spain). It was ruled by the Visigoths but not effectively controlled by them because they were divided by dynastic disputes. To an Arab

army accustomed to success, Hispania looked like easy prey.

In 711 CE, general Tariq ibn-Ziyad crossed the straits with a combined Arab-Berber force and seized the rock that bears his name—Gibraltar, from the Arabic *Gibr al-Tariq* (Rock of Tariq). In the traditional account, Tariq's first act on landing was to burn the invasion fleet. He told his 12,000-strong army: "You have nowhere to run to—behind you is the sea and in front of you is the enemy!"

In the eighth century CE, Arab warriors established a lasting Muslim tradition throughout northern Africa. This photograph shows the old souk (market) in the holy city of Kairouan, Tunisia.

Gibraltar stands at the southern tip of the Iberian Peninsula within sight of Africa.

King Roderick of the Visigoths had assembled a great army, but it was put to the sword by the invaders at the Battle of Guadalete (a river near present-day Cádiz, Spain). Roderick either died or fled, and the few surviving members of his government took refuge near Seville. The Arabs then besieged the city, which quickly capitulated. Visigothic resistance was in tatters. A second Arab army arrived from Africa, and within five years, the invaders conquered almost the whole of the Iberian Peninsula for Islam. Only the far northern part of Spain remained free of Arab influence. The small kingdoms that sprang up in the north would, centuries later, provide the springboard for a Christian reconquest of the Iberian Peninsula.

Having established themselves in Spain, the armies of Islam turned their attention to the very fertile lands that stretched out northward beyond the Pyrenees Mountains. There was no rea-son for the invaders to assume that the Franks, who ruled there, could resist them any better than the vanquished Visigoths had done. Arab bands began plundering Aquitaine, and the local Christian population soon came to expect Islamic raids on their territory. In 732 CE, however, a great army of Arab horsemen appeared on the plains of Aquitaine. It was clear that, this time, the Arabs were set for conquering rather than just raiding.

The Franks, however, were much better equipped than the Visigoths had been to resist the Arab army. While the Visigothic forces had been divided by parochial rivalries, the Franks were united by an outstanding military leader, Charles Martel (Charles the Hammer).

This painting of the Battle of Guadalete (in which the Arabs defeated the Visigoths) is the work of Spanish painter Salvador Martínez Cubells (1842–1914 CE).

The Arabs won the first victory, defeating Duke Odo of Aquitaine at the Battle of the River Garonne—a bloody clash in which, so the Christian chroniclers lamented, "God only would know the number slaughtered." Odo then summoned Charles Martel, who first encountered the invaders at an unknown location in Aquitaine, somewhere between Tours and Poitiers. After seven days of reconnaissance, the Arabs attacked on October 10, 732 CE. The determined Franks simply stood their ground, beating off the invaders, holding fast, and making no attempt to pursue the Arabs when they fell back into their own ranks. The Frankish lines were still unbroken at sunset. As night fell, the fighting ended for the day. At dawn, the Franks were surprised to find themselves alone; the Arabs had disappeared under cover of darkness.

LEO III, THE ICONOCLAST

The Byzantine emperor Leo III (ruled 717–741 CE) was a formidable ruler who left a wide and enduring legacy. The Isaurian dynasty that he founded held power in Constantinople until 802 CE. Leo established a legal code called the *Ecloga*, which remained in use for 200 years. In 730 CE, Leo banned the use of images in Christian worship. The policy, known as iconoclasm—from the Greek *eikon* (image) and *klaien* (break)—appalled the church authorities. The eastern patriarch Germanos I resigned in protest and was replaced with one of Leo's supporters. In 732 CE, Pope Gregory II excommunicated the emperor and thus accelerated the separation of the eastern and western Christian churches, which became permanent in the 11th century CE. Leo III repelled the Arab siege of Constantinople and established his empire as a bulwark against Islamic expansionism. He completed his reign with successful military campaigns in Asia Minor.

This painting by French artist Charles Steuben (1788–1856 CE) is an imaginative re-creation of Charles Martel's victory over Arab forces at the Battle of Tours.

GREEK FIRE

Greek fire was an incendiary weapon. Sources suggest that it was invented in Constantinople during the reign of the emperor Constantine IV (ruled 668–685 CE) by a Greek-speaking refugee from the Arab conquest of Syria.

Although the Byzantines kept the composition of Greek fire a closely guarded secret, it is now known to have been made of naphtha, an easily combustible petroleum ether. The Byzantines used burning cloths to ignite the sticky liquid and then threw it (in pots) or sprayed it (from tubes) onto enemy vessels. According to contemporary accounts, the fires thus started could not be extinguished with water; only urine or sand could put them out. Greek fire inflicted great damage on the Arab fleet during the siege of Constantinople in 717 CE.

The Battle of Tours (also known as the Battle of Poitiers) was a turning point; after that defeat, the Arabs advanced no farther. However, the Frankish victory did not put an end to Islamic incursions.

Fighting between the Christians and Muslims continued sporadically for more than 200 years, particularly in Roussillon, where, for long periods, Arab raids made normal civilian life almost impossible. After the 10th century CE, the Christians in northern Spain began to retrieve the lands to the south at the start of the Reconquista (Reclamation). Their struggle against the Arab occupiers of southern and central Iberia shaped Spanish and Portuguese history for the rest of the Middle Ages.

Conquest in the east

In Asia, the Arabs, having consolidated their power in Persia, marched eastward along the route once taken by Alexander the Great. They captured Kabul in 664 CE and reached the Indus River by 712 CE, the year after Tariq ibn–Ziyad invaded Spain. In the north, the Arabs took parts of Turkestan, captured the city of Samarkand in 710 CE, and finally reached the Chinese border.

Meanwhile, the Arabs, breaking the naval dominance of the Byzantines in the eastern Mediterranean, sent raiders to terrorize Christians living on the coast and expelled the Byzantine emperor from Cyprus. On land, however, the Byzantine Empire stood firm against the onslaughts of the Muslim warriors. The empire had been reduced to the Balkan Peninsula and Asia Minor, but there its soldiers held on with the strength of desperation. In 674 CE, the Arabs attempted to take Constantinople, but the city defended itself. The siege went on for five years; each spring, the Arabs turned up to fight for the city but were driven back. In maintaining their defense, the Byzantines made use of a new weapon, Greek fire.

The Arabs besieged Constantinople again in 717 CE. The city was ruled at that point by Leo III (see box, page 761), who had recently deposed Theodosius III, ending a series of succession disputes that had weakened the empire for many years. Leo was a superb military tactician as well as a skilled political leader and diplomat. He won the Bulgarians to his cause, and they attacked the Arab army successfully. Leo demonstrated his tactical genius by stretching a heavy chain underwater across the Golden Horn; scores of Arab ships were caught on the chain and then torched by Greek fire. The Arabs retreated, and the siege of Constantinople was lifted. Although the Arabs continued to raid Anatolia, they did not again attack the Byzantine capital.

See also:

The Caliphate (volume 6, page 764) •
Mohammed and Islam (volume 6, page 736) •
The Riches of Islam (volume 6, page 776)

Modern Spain is a Roman Catholic country, but its architecture still shows strong Arab influence. This is a shopping arcade in the southern city of Seville.

THE CALIPHATE

Between the 7th and 13th centuries CE, Islam's ruling caliphate was controlled successively by four Arab dynasties before falling to the Mongols. The caliphate later reverted to Muslim control under the Ottoman Turks.

In 656 CE, the assassination of Othman ibn Affan, the third caliph (successor to the prophet Mohammed) sparked a bitter succession contest. The two rival claimants were the prophet's grandson Hassan and Mu'awiyah, a prominent member of the same Umayyad clan of caravan merchants to which Othman himself had belonged. Having triumphed in the ensuing struggle, Mu'awiyah established in 661 CE the first great caliphate dynasty, named Umayyad after his clan.

Mu'awiyah moved the capital of the recently formed Islamic Empire to Damascus, Syria, while Hassan retired to Medina (the City of the Prophet), where Mohammed had established Islam (in 620–630 CE). Henceforth, Medina became established as a holy city in Islam, away from the centers of political power, its sites visited by pilgrims, scholars, and wealthy potential successors to Hassan. In contrast, Mu'awiyah's establishment of his seat of government in Damascus gave Muslims significantly greater exposure to the developed culture and ways of government of the Byzantine Empire.

Mu'awiyah ruled for two decades (661–680 CE). During that time, he laid the groundwork for a political system that dominated the Islamic world for the next 500 years. Mu'awiyah's use of power resembled that of a potentate in the capitals of Byzantine Constantinople or Persian Ctesiphon more than it did that of the prophet Mohammed or Caliph Omar (ruled 634–644 CE). Mu'awiyah ruled through and with the aid of a group of favorites who obtained their positions not by ability but through flattery and family connections; corruption and intrigue were endemic at the court of the Umayyads. Nevertheless, Mu'awiyah was a talented sovereign, capable of assessing problems quickly and of taking decisive action whenever it was needed. His orders were carried out by civilians and military personnel alike.

The Umayyad caliphate

There were no succession problems after Mu'awiyah's death in 680 CE because the caliph had previously named his son, Yazid, as his successor, thereby setting a precedent that would be followed by his descendants. Dynastic succession certainly increased the stability of the empire, but it provoked objections among the majority of Muslims, the Sunnis. The Sunnis argued that—following the practice established by Mohammed's first four successors—the caliph should be

One of the holiest shrines of Islam, the Umayyad Mosque, or Grand Mosque, in Damascus, Syria, was completed in 715 CE.

THE ISLAMIC WORLD IN THE EIGHTH CENTURY CE

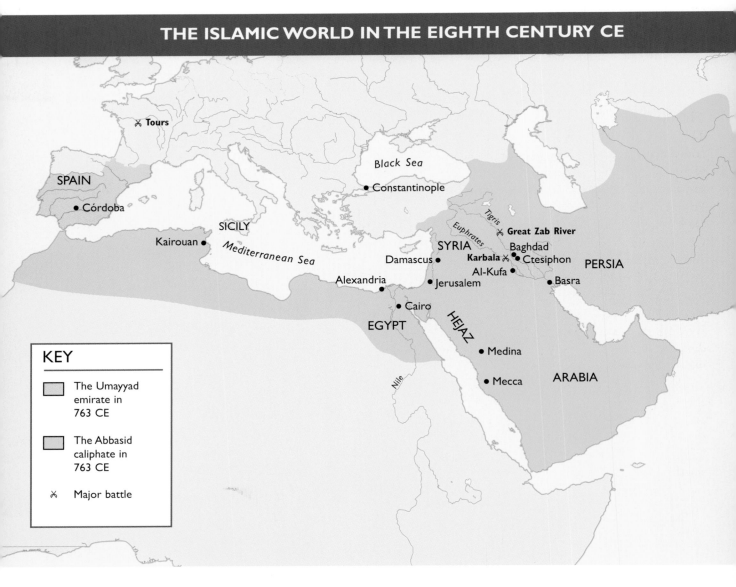

a member of the Quaraish tribe of Mohammed and that he should be elected by a council of Muslim elders.

The Sunnis also insisted that the caliph should enforce Koranic law and foster the spread of Islam. The Umayyads failed to satisfy either requirement. Scandalous stories circulated about the ruling dynasty, which acquired a reputation for degeneracy. At the court in Damascus, a sophisticated, cosmopolitan atmosphere reigned, which was quite at odds with Muslim orthodoxy. For example, Islam forbids the consumption of alcohol, but under Mu'awiyah's son,

Yazid I, wine was in common use in the palace; one prince was said to be accustomed to swimming in wine. Traditional Islamic opinion was also hostile to the Umayyads' failure to discriminate in favor of Muslims; the rulers appointed Christians to high administrative positions, and they were happy to patronize non-Islamic artists. The court poet Al-Akhtal (640–710 CE), for example, was a Monophysite Christian. (Monophysitism—from the Greek *monos*, "single," and *physis*, "nature"—contended that Jesus Christ had a single, wholly divine nature; this was at odds not only with the

Christian doctrine that Christ was simultaneously both human and divine, but also with the Islamic belief that Jesus was an entirely human prophet with no divine element to his person.)

The glory of Damascus

The tolerance shown at the Umayyad court may have been seen as moral laxity by orthodox Muslims, but it created room for the growth of Arabian culture. Poetry, art, and architecture flourished in Damascus in the late seventh century CE. Umayyad architects transformed a Byzantine church said to contain the body of John the Baptist into a mosque that remains one of the most beautiful in western Asia. Artists, including some Byzantines, added flowing decorative designs to the palaces and homes of the wealthiest residents.

The city of Damascus, which under the Byzantines had been no more than an important fortress, became the center of a great world empire that by around 715 CE stretched all the way across northern Africa to Spain. Vast numbers of merchant caravans passed through the city, giving a great boost to trade and craftsmanship. On the main street of Damascus, huge sums changed hands. While the merchants grew rich, the weavers of Damascus developed new techniques that made it possible to produce a firm, lustrous, patterned fabric named Damask that is still in use today. Yet, although Damascus seemed to have a glittering future, the rule of the Umayyads was short-lived. The dynasty founded by Mu'awiyah succumbed to revolution, and imperial power shifted eastward to a new metropolis: Baghdad.

Challenge to Umayyad power

Mu'awiyah's son, Yazid I, reigned for three years (680–683 CE). The succession conflict that had dogged the beginning of Mu'awiyah's reign flared up

again; Yazid was challenged by revolts in Mecca and among the Shi'ites of Al-Kufa in Mesopotamia (part of modern Iraq). Both rebel groups backed the rival claim to the caliphate of Hussein, Ali's second son and the grandson of Mohammed. (The split between Sunni and Shi'ite Muslims that arose as a result of these early disputes over succession to the caliphate has endured even into the 21st century CE.)

Yazid killed Hussein at the Battle of Karbala in 680 CE, but the Meccan rebellion continued until it was finally put down by the caliph Abd al-Malik,

The Umayyad Mosque in Damascus, Syria, contains a wealth of beautiful decorations, including this intricate mosaic in a pavilion in the arcade courtyard.

(ruled 685–705 CE). During the conflict (685–691 CE), Abd al-Malik built the Dome of the Rock, a mosque in Jerusalem, as a new pilgrimage site to discourage Islamic pilgrims from traveling to rebel-held Mecca. Abd al-Malik also succeeded in reuniting Umayyad holdings in Iraq, Syria, and Palestine in 691 CE, and in the next year, he recaptured Mecca. His son Al-Walid (ruled 705–715 CE) oversaw the Arabs' permanent expansion into northern Africa, the conversion to Islam of the Berber peoples of the region, and the capture of Spain from the Visigoths.

However, the Umayyads never firmly established themselves; even at the height of their power, they remained vulnerable. The dynasty's problems increased as its taxation policies created widespread unrest, even among their own followers.

They undertook a jihad, or holy war, against the Byzantine Empire, but that enterprise foundered. Far away in Aquitaine (southwestern France), their expansion from Spain into central and northern Europe was halted by Charles Martel and his Frankish army at the Battle of Tours in 732 CE.

Meanwhile, a group of recent non-Arab converts to Islam began to express dissatisfaction at their low status within the Islamic state. Called the *mawali* in Arabic, they complained that they were treated as second-rate Muslims. Their rebellion gained support in the Hejaz region (on the east coast of the Red Sea and containing Mecca and Medina) and in Persia, where large numbers of people had abandoned the ancient Persian religion of Zoroastrianism for Islam.

The Dome of the Rock in Jerusalem is built on land that is sacred to Muslims, Jews, and Christians.

No matter how forceful the leadership of the Umayyads was and how quickly the economy developed, the division caused by the manner of their accession to power and the defeat of the followers of Ali repeatedly resurfaced. The Shi'ites, who would not allow the defeat of Ali and his sons to be forgotten, aimed for a restoration of the old caliphate. Time and again, the Umayyads were forced to subdue uprisings; in the garrison cities of Al-Kufa and Basra, soldiers lived under constant threat. The Hejaz region grew increasingly restless as the Shi'ites gained followers.

Tribal and dynastic conflicts that had long plagued Arab armies began to escalate. Each succession in the palace of Damascus prompted violent incidents, including the murders of soldiers in even the most distant and inaccessible garrison towns. The last Umayyads lacked the skill to keep these battling forces in balance, and their empire began to disintegrate.

The rise of the Abbasids

In this volatile atmosphere, new contenders emerged for the succession to the caliphate. The new contenders, the Abbasids, were cousins of the Umayyads and claimed descent from Abbas, an uncle of the prophet Mohammed. Increasing numbers of Muslims in the empire began to favor a handover of power to the Abbasids. In Persia, Abu Muslim—a convert to Islam and a fervent Shi'ite—began to use the prospect of a change of ruling family to stir up the population. In 747 CE, Abu Muslim and a group of Persian converts joined with non-Muslim groups dissatisfied with Umayyad rule to declare Abu al-Abbas, an Abbasid, as caliph. With significant support in northern Persia, the rebels defeated the Umayyad caliph, Marwan II, at the Battle of the Great Zab River (now in Iraq) on January 25, 750 CE. Marwan fled and was killed a few months later in Egypt.

This gold dinar was minted in 696 CE during the reign of the Umayyad caliph Abd al-Malik.

THE DOME OF THE ROCK

The Umayyad caliph Abd al-Malik (ruled 685–705 CE) had the Dome of the Rock built in Jerusalem between 685 and 691 CE. The Dome is a mosque built as a *mashhad* (pilgrimage shrine) and is the oldest surviving Islamic monument. It stands around a rock sacred to both Jews and Muslims. Muslims believe that the rock is the place from which the prophet Mohammed ascended to heaven during his miraculous night journey from Mecca. Around 620 CE, according to Islamic tradition, Mohammed was at prayer one night beside the Kaaba in Mecca when he was taken up by the angel Gabriel, transported to Jerusalem, greeted by an assembly of prophets, and allowed to ascend a golden ladder to heaven. Jews believe that the rock was the place in which Abraham prepared to sacrifice his son Isaac to God and where Jacob had his dream of a ladder ascending to heaven; its location is also important because it stands on Temple Mount, the site of the ancient Temple of Solomon. Celebrated as one of the finest achievements of world architecture, the Dome of the Rock was built by Byzantine architects. Its dome is 65 feet (20 m) tall and the same size across. It soars above a circular arrangement of 16 columns and piers set within an octagonal walkway containing 24 columns and piers. Its outer walls are also octagonal. Pilgrims pray in the adjacent Al-Aqsa Mosque.

THE UMAYYADS IN CÓRDOBA

When the first Abassid caliph, Abu al-Abbas, attempted to wipe out his Umayyad predecessors, only one prominent member of the Umayyad clan, Abd ar-Rahman, escaped. Fleeing westward, Abd ar-Rahman reached Muslim-held Spain, where he ousted the provincial governor of Córdoba by force of arms.

In Córdoba, Abd ar-Rahman established a dynasty that ruled until 1031 CE. At first, the Umayyads coexisted with the ruling Abbasids; Abd ar-Rahman recognized the Abbasids' right to the caliphate, and the Abbasids made no effort to prove their might in Spain. The Spanish territories were in some sense the price that Abu al-Abbas was willing to pay for the caliphate. The Umayyads, while resenting the rule of the new dynasty in Baghdad and still believing that their family had a right to the caliphate, made no

challenge. However, when the realm of the Abbasids collapsed into anarchy in the 10th century CE, the Umayyads at last put their presumptions into practice. In 929 CE, Abd ar-Rahman III named himself the caliph of Córdoba.

The caliphate of Córdoba collapsed less than a century later, as Spain fragmented into rival Islamic states. Over the 150-odd years that followed, Christians were able to reconquer the entire Iberian Peninsula. By around 1200 CE, the Reconquista (Reclamation) was almost complete—although it was not until 1492 CE that the last Muslim sovereign, the ruler of Granada, was forced to withdraw to northern Africa.

Built during the reign of Abd ar-Rahmon III, the Mezquita (mosque) in Córdoba was converted to a Christian cathedral after the Reconquista.

Abu al-Abbas assumed the caliphate and proved himself to be the most ruthless of operators, eliminating not only leading Umayyads but also rival Abbasid figures and earning himself the title As-Saffah (the Bloodshedder). Under his rule, the Umayyads were almost entirely wiped out; the only prominent member of the tribe to escape was Abd ar-Rahman, who fled to Córdoba in Spain and created an Umayyad dynasty that remained in power there until 1031 CE.

Abu al-Abbas had gained his power with Shi'ite support, but he did not put Shi'ite ideals into practice. He took whatever action he considered to be politically expedient. He ruled for only four years, and after his death in 754 CE, it initially appeared that his dynasty would not last. A bitter civil war broke out in which Abu Muslim fought on the same side as Al-Mansur, Abu al-Abbas's brother and successor. Largely because of Abu Muslim's military prowess, Al-Mansur was able to take over as caliph. Yet, once in office, apparently fearing Abu Muslim's potential as a rival, Al-Mansur had Abu Muslim killed.

Al-Mansur's City of Peace

Al-Mansur moved the imperial capital to Mesopotamia, where the Umayyads had many enemies. There, beside the Tigris River, he built a metropolis that he called Madinat as-Salam (City of Peace). However, the poetic name did not catch on, and most people still called the place by its former name, Baghdad.

The relocation of the capital city was more than symbolic. Baghdad is significantly farther than Damascus from the Arabian deserts in which Islam was born and considerably closer to Persia. Al-Mansur did not make the mistake of alienating Persian converts to Islam.

This wood engraving from the 19th century CE depicts Harun al-Rashid, the fifth Abbasid caliph.

Some historians have suggested that the Abbasid conquest was actually a Persian victory. However, while it is true that there were many Persian ceremonies at the caliph's court in Baghdad and that Persians won a significant amount of power under the Abbasids, there was no question of a Persian takeover. Baghdad was always an Arabian city. Its people, like its caliph and courtiers, spoke Arabic, not Persian.

Al-Mansur was an energetic administrator who consolidated the power of the caliphate and reorganized the imperial bureaucracy. He initiated a policy of cultural tolerance that attempted to unite his subjects on the basis of their shared religion rather than forcing an Arabic

771

civilization on them. Contending that all believers were equal before God, Al-Mansur treated no one inequitably.

Abbasid achievements

The Abbasids encouraged education and the arts, inviting foreign intellectuals to their court for lectures and debates. The dynasty reached its peak during the caliphate of Harun al-Rashid (ruled 786–809 CE). Al-Rashid was an able diplomat who exchanged ambassadors with Charlemagne, king of the Franks (ruled 768–814 CE) and the first Holy Roman emperor (ruled 800–814 CE).

On his death, Al-Rashid attempted to divide power between his sons, leaving Al-Amin in control in Baghdad and Al-Mamun in power in the eastern empire. However, this arrangement quickly broke down. The resulting civil war culminated in the siege of Baghdad by supporters of Al-Mamun in 812 CE. After the fall of the city and the death of his brother, Al-Mamun became sole ruler from 813 to 833 CE.

Al-Mamun faced difficulties with Sunni Muslims. Sunnis believed that the Koran was the eternal word of God revealed to Mohammed and that it was eternally existing with God and so was uncreated by him. However, Al-Mamun was influenced by the Islamic theological sect of the Mutazilites, who held that while the word of God was part of him and so was eternally existing in him, the Koran was an expression of the word and was created by God.

Al-Mamun responded to the problem by removing Sunnis from the civil service. He achieved that through a sort of inquisition, in which he made all officials swear that the Koran had been created. Al-Mamun established a golden age of science and literature. As he gradually yielded educational, political, and administrative control to the functionaries whose positions he had established, he

This painting by Julius Köckert (1827–1918 CE) is an imaginative evocation of the historic meeting between Harun al-Rashid and the emperor Charlemagne.

took an increasingly active, personal role in protecting his own concept of Islam from heretical attack.

Unity and regional differences

In the ninth century CE, the Arab world was large and full of contradictions. Generally, the caliphs allowed diverse cultures or peoples within the empire to function independently. In spite of the unifying influence of religion and language, regional differences remained significant. Arabic dialects had already diversified so much that an Arab from Africa could not understand an Arab from Iraq. However, the written language remained the same throughout the empire, from India to Spain. Modern observers are amazed at the extent of unity that was maintained. Rarely has such a heterogeneous world been kept together successfully for so long.

Abbasid decline

After the death of Al-Mamun in 833 CE, his successors as caliph continued his practice of delegating administrative authority to government officials while themselves taking a prominent role in religious life. They regarded themselves as defenders of Islam and encouraged the persecution of nonbelievers. The caliphs became increasingly resented outside Baghdad, and their political power began to decline severely.

In the eastern provinces, a number of rebel leaders declared independence and established their own principalities. In northern Africa, the Shi'ites established their own caliphate (see box, page 774). The empire effectively shrank to the region of what is now Iraq and then to Baghdad as rebel slaves took over the southern part of the country.

By the mid-10th century CE, the caliphs were no longer strong enough to rule alone and could remain in power only for as long as they retained the sup-

port of their military commanders. In 945 CE, the Shi'ite Buyids—originally tribesmen from western Iran—took power in Baghdad. They kept the Abbasid caliphs in position but only as figureheads; henceforth, the caliphs' tasks were no more than ceremonial. In 1055 CE, the Buyids were replaced by the Seljuk Turks, Muslims who came originally from the northern edge of the Islamic world around the Caspian and Aral seas. The Seljuks also allowed the caliphs to remain in office. However, under the Turkish sultans, the Abbasids retained even less influence than they had had under the Buyids. The Shi'ites fought a vigorous guerrilla campaign against the Seljuks and the Abbasids.

This pyx (small round container) was carved from ivory in Córdoba in the 10th century CE. The ornamental relief depicts the pleasures of life at the Islamic court.

THE FATIMIDS AND THE RISE OF CAIRO

In the 10th century CE, militant Shi'ites established a counter-caliphate in northern Africa. They were members of the Ismai'li sect of Shi'ites and refused to recognize the authority of the Abbasid caliphs. The dynasty was established in Tunis in 909 CE by Ubayd Allah, who claimed to be a descendant of Fatima (daughter of the prophet Mohammed) and called his dynasty the Fatimid. Ubayd Allah's followers believed that he and his descendants were the rightful caliphs because of their descent from Fatima and her husband Ali; their aim was not to set up a new power base of their own but to replace the Abbasids as rulers of all Islamic territories.

The Fatimids acquired a large following in northern Africa. They took control of Egypt and established a new capital city at Cairo on the Nile River near the old town of Fustat. The official year of Cairo's establishment was 969 CE. In that year, the Fatimids reached the apex of their power, while Iraq was being torn apart by fratricidal struggles among the Seljuk Turks. The new city of Cairo rose quickly to prominence. Baghdad was decaying rapidly, and the power of the caliph there was negligible; Damascus was unable to regain its former position. Cairo became a metropolis, to the delight of the Fatimids, who were eager to make their empire the center of all Islam. When an earthquake destroyed the harbor city of Siraf in the Persian Gulf, traders were forced to divert their shipping routes to the Red Sea, much closer to Cairo, and Fatimid commerce benefited greatly. The caliphate of the Fatimids was less glorious than that of the Abbasids or the Umayyads. The Fatimid caliph in Cairo was unable to maintain order without the use of mercenaries. Yet by the end of the 10th century CE, at the height of the caliphate's power, the Fatimids controlled northern Africa from Egypt westward to what is now Algeria, together with the eastern Mediterranean coast to Syria and the island of Sicily.

Because of their claim to be descended from Fatima and Ali, the Fatimids considered themselves to be in possession of divine truth; their imams (spiritual leaders) were said to be sinless and infallible. Fatimid missionaries roamed the Muslim world, seeking converts; that made them a theological and political threat to the Sunni Abbasid caliphate in Baghdad. The Fatimids were overthrown by Saladin, sultan of Egypt, in 1171 CE.

Built in the ninth century CE, the Mosque of Ahmad ibn Tulun is Cairo's oldest place of worship.

This Persian book illumination from the 14th century CE depicts the siege of Baghdad in 1258 CE by the forces of Hulagu Khan.

Ultimately, the downfall of the Abbasid dynasty came not from the Shi'ites but from forces quite foreign to the Middle Eastern world. In 1258 CE, the Mongol leader Hulagu Khan, grandson of Genghis Khan, sacked Baghdad, ending five centuries of Abbasid rule. Two members of the Abbasid dynasty—Al-Mustansir and Al-Hakim—escaped to Egypt, where they were given a guarded welcome by the Mamluk sultan Baybars I. (The Mamluks were former slave-soldiers in Muslim armies in northern Africa; they established a dynasty that had control over Syria and Egypt from 1250 to 1517 CE.) Baybars I named them both, in succession, as caliph but made sure that they had only religious authority and no political influence.

The caliphate in later years

The caliphs lost everything as almost the whole Arab world fell to Ottoman (Turkish) conquest. Wherever Muslim rule prevailed, competing kings called themselves caliph but made no attempt to carry out the responsibilities that had originally gone with the title. In the great empire established by the Ottoman Turks (which lasted from the 14th century CE to 1922 CE), the title of caliph was common but was stressed only for its religious importance when the ruling sultans wanted the united backing of Muslims against their Christian enemies. After World War I (1914–1918 CE) brought down the Ottomans, Turkish nationalists overthrew both the sultanate and the caliphate. The Grand National Assembly of Turkey formally abolished the caliphate in 1924 CE. Subsequently, the title of caliph (as well as direct descent from the prophet Mohammed) was claimed by Husayn ibn Al, king of the Hejaz, the region conquered in 1925 CE by Abdul Aziz ibn Saud and now part of Saudi Arabia. There has been no international Muslim consensus on reestablishing a caliphate.

See also:

Mohammed and Islam (volume 6, page 736) •
The Riches of Islam (volume 6, page 776) •
The Rise of Islam (volume 6, page 752)

THE RICHES OF ISLAM

Between the 8th and 13th centuries CE, the caliphate that governed the Islamic world oversaw a period of cultural and intellectual achievement that was unprecedented. The period was the finest flowering of Islamic culture.

Mu'awiyah, who founded Islam's first great caliphate dynasty in 661 CE, belonged to the Umayyads, a merchant clan. He changed the priority of the caliphs from religious idealism—honoring and preserving the prophet Mohammed's legacy—to mercantilism and trade.

The Arabs had conquered a prosperous part of the world. Their expansion was, to a great extent, at the expense of Persia and Byzantium—two empires that had previously formed cohesive wholes and avoided disintegration into self-contained, competitive areas. Half of the territory in these rich and well-developed states fell into Arab hands within only a few years. The conquerors were able to take over their new holdings with little difficulty and soon integrated the acquisitions into a new empire. The Arabs were certainly able to get their empire off to a better start than the Franks managed in war-plagued Gaul.

The caliphs were strong and powerful rulers who saw to it that the enormous empire was governed effectively. Their territory eventually extended from the mouth of the Tagus River at Lisbon in the west to the unassailable border fortresses of China in the east. They built safe roads and a trading network that covered vast distances. Even the civil wars that plagued the Islamic world did not disrupt its economic traffic.

By camel across the desert

While the residents of maritime lands or riverside areas saw the desert as a dangerous and impenetrable barrier, for the Bedouin and other Islamic merchants, it was a connecting road. The deserts of the east became the arteries of the Arabs' immense empire. Caravan stations—places for rest and feeding—lay along all the main routes, roughly one day's journey apart. At busy points, the stations developed into desert towns, with large pavilions and many inns for travelers. Some of these stations, including the one near Aleppo (in modern Syria), still exist.

A caravan's destination would generally be one of the great commercial centers of the Arab world: Baghdad, Damascus, Samarra, or Cairo. In those cities, merchandise was traded—often continuing its long voyage in another merchant's caravan. There was lively trade with India, and the Islamic merchants of Turkestan had dealings with Chinese traders who brought their silks through the Gobi Desert into central Asia.

Islamic merchants did not fear the desert. The sand dunes of Arabia and the Sahara Desert were familiar territory to Muslim believers, who knew how to

This illustration of a merchant ship at sea comes from a 13th-century-CE Arabic manuscript.

القرآن ثم وابعد اساطير بلدها وزخارف جلالها وقال اركبوا فيها بسم الله مجراها

ومرساها ثم نفس نفس المغرمين او عباد الله للكرمين وقال اما انا

THE SHIP OF THE DESERT

The rapid growth of Islamic trade was rooted not only in the ingenuity of Arab traders but also in the strength and bravery of the camel, "the ship of the desert" (so called because of its rolling gait, which makes human riders feel as if they are in a boat on the sea). The Bedouin of Arabia owed their lives and livelihoods to their camels. They were the first people to tame the animal, which they knew as an extremely tough creature that could survive in the driest of areas.

The camel is outstandingly suited to serving humans in the desert. Although it does not actually live on less water than other animals, it needs to drink much less often than they do. It can easily go for three or four days without taking in water and has been known to survive for 17 days without a drink. The camel can lose 25 percent of its body weight through dehydration; in any other animal, such privation would cause lethal thickening of the blood. When a camel gets the chance to "refuel," it does so very quickly—being capable of drinking 25 gallons (100 l) of water in 10 minutes. Camels can survive on sparse, thorny vegetation, including twigs. The camel has long legs and soft, widespread feet perfectly adapted for walking on sand. To protect it from sandstorms, the camel has two rows of eyelashes on each eye and protective hair in its ears; it can also close its nostrils. As a beast of burden, the camel is without equal, capable of carrying up to 220 pounds (100 kg) on its back for weeks at a time. It is useful in other ways, as well. The female camel produces milk with a high fat content. The camel's meat is edible, and camel hide can be made into warm blankets that are essential to the Bedouin in the cold desert nights. Even the camel's dung is useful, because it burns easily in an evening fire.

There are two species of camel. The Bactrian camel has two humps and is found in central Asia. The Arabian camel of the Middle East and Africa has only one hump. The Bactrian camel is a little smaller than the Arabian camel.

Bedouin people lead a train of camels through the desert.

survive with little water in the burning sun. The Arabs had also tamed the camel and learned to use it as a means of travel across inhospitable lands.

Traders had discovered the value of camels very early, using them in long caravans for safety and greater profit. The political unity that the Arabs brought to such a large area helped the development of caravan traffic. There was no longer a restless Persian-Byzantine border, and even more important was the fact that the Persian and Byzantine tax collectors had been banished; the taxes levied by the caliphs were almost a relief after the oppressive system imposed by previous rulers.

A well-organized caravan operated with military efficiency. Its leader and a few of his aids had unlimited authority; the rules of the trail were precisely formulated and just as precisely followed. Only in emergencies could a caravan deviate from the designated route, because, away from the beaten track, the relentless heat, the lack of water, and the blowing sand were too treacherous to tackle. Before a caravan set out on a journey across the desert, its members prayed for safe passage. Along the route, expedition leaders would pay desert dwellers not to attack their caravans; the payments were known as tolls, but may equally well be described as protection money.

Piracy and trade on the high seas

The desert was not the only Islamic trade route; the sea was equally important. Shortly after the death of the prophet Mohammed, the first Arabs traveled to the Mediterranean Sea, which, at the time, was dominated by Byzantine war-

Le Livre des Parfums   Chap. VII

OFFICINE ET LABORATOIRE D'UN PARFUMEUR CHIMISTE ARABE
AU 12ème SIÈCLE
D'après un manuscrit Arabe Persan de l'époque

ships. The Arabs' original aim was to plunder. At first, most Muslims viewed the earliest sea expeditions as recklessness, but the rich spoils brought back by the raiders made even the greatest skeptics change their minds.

The Arabs soon became a maritime force to be reckoned with, ousting the Byzantine fleets from the western Mediterranean. In the east, meanwhile,

This diptych from an illuminated 12th-century-CE manuscript shows a tradesman making and selling perfume, one of the most lucrative commodities in the medieval Arab world.

779

This illustration of Sindbad and the Old Man of the Sea, from One Thousand and One Nights, *is by British artist Arthur Rackham (1867–1939 CE).*

the Byzantines could barely defend their own coasts. Even in the Aegean Sea—a Byzantine stronghold for so long—Muslim fleets raided Christian trade ships and earned a fearsome reputation as pirates. Effectively, the Muslims ruled the seas, and their fleets could plunder without opposition. Once, Arab sailors even put in at Ostia, the port of Rome at the mouth of the Tiber River. The local residents did not dare to confront the invaders; the response to the threat of repeated attacks was to build watchtowers so the locals could see the ships in time to clear the area.

However, the Arabs did not confine their maritime activities to piracy. They soon began sending legitimate trade ships across the Mediterranean and established a number of Muslim harbors. There was little commerce between Muslims and Christians; relations were far too strained for peaceful trade. In any case, plundering the ships of nonbelievers was more profitable to the Arabs than dealing with Christian merchants. Such trade as there was between Muslims and western European Christians was conducted via traveling Jewish merchants.

The greatest volume of Muslim maritime trade was carried out across the Indian Ocean. Huge fleets sailed from the Persian Gulf to the coast of India; loaded with valuable spices, the ships then sailed back to their home harbors. These were adventurous voyages that generated tall tales. The account of Sindbad the Sailor in *One Thousand and One Nights* is one such story.

Arab craft products

The Arabs in the years of the caliphate were skillful craftspeople. Generally not satisfied with traditional production methods, the Arabs looked for improvements. One result was the windmill, an invention that saved an enormous amount of human energy; work that had previously been carried out on labor-intensive treadmills could now be performed by means of a simple mechanism that harnessed atmospheric energy. The first windmills, which used vertical shafts and horizontally moving blades, were developed in Islamic Persia by the early 10th century CE.

In Islamic Spain, smithing developed into a true art. Swords from Córdoba and Toledo in Spain became famous throughout the Islamic world; they were feared by

Christians and traded in Africa. Woven textiles from Islamic cities were without equal. Even the studios of Byzantium could not outperform the weavers of Damascus and Mosul. Carpet making reached a peak of perfection in Persia and Anatolia; carpets in beautiful colors and patterns made their way from small villages to the palaces of the mighty. Carpet production supported the dye industry, which was concentrated particularly in the Persian Gulf port of Basra (now in Iraq).

Arab philosophy and learning

Among the greatest riches of the years of the caliphate was its legacy of learning. Although Persia, India, and Egypt all influenced the development of Arab philosophy and science, it was the Greek

The design on this glazed plate, made in Egypt in the 11th century CE, shows a seated figure holding a drinking vessel in each hand.

ONE THOUSAND AND ONE NIGHTS

The collection of tales entitled *One Thousand and One Nights* is probably the most widely known piece of Arabic literature. It features the celebrated narratives of Aladdin, Ali Baba and the Forty Thieves, and Sindbad the Sailor's Seven Voyages. It is a compendium of popular tales that were passed on orally for many centuries before they were written down, perhaps in the eighth and ninth centuries CE. The written collection appears to have developed from an Arabic translation of a Persian anthology but incorporates a great range of folk material and narratives from India, Turkey, Iraq, and Egypt as well as Iran. It also includes Islamic religious stories. The oldest fragment of the work, written in Arabic and found in what is now Syria, dates from the ninth century CE. In 947 CE, the author

Al-Masudi referred to a Persian work called *The Thousand Tales*, noting that it was popularly known as *A Thousand Nights*.

The framework of the stories is as follows. Shahryar, king of Persia, is outraged by his wife's infidelity and has her executed. He then marries a new bride every day and has her executed the following morning. He is eventually thwarted by a young woman named Scheherazade, who tells him stories every night but always leaves them unfinished, so he will not know how they end until the following evening. Shahryar postpones her execution again and again and eventually abandons his scheme. The fifth Abbasid caliph, Harun al-Rashid (ruled 786–809 CE), appears in several tales, along with his vizier, Jafar al-Barmaki.

philosophers of the classical period who had the greatest effect on Islamic scholarship in the Middle Ages.

The study of science, mathematics, and philosophy was encouraged in Baghdad by the early Abbasid caliphs, particularly in the Bayt al-Hikma (House of Wisdom) founded by the caliph Al-Mamun (ruled 813–833 CE). The Bayt al-Hikma was modeled on the imperial library of the Persian Sassanid Empire; numerous works on medicine, agriculture, mathematics, and astrology were translated from Persian and Syriac into Arabic. Al-Mamun was a great patron of the arts and sciences, and he encouraged the study of ancient Greek philosophy. According to Muslim chronicles, the

Greek philosopher Aristotle appeared before the caliph in a dream, advising him to study Greek science. Al-Mamun enthusiastically complied and began to collect ancient manuscripts; he dispatched emissaries to Constantinople to find the writings of Plato, Aristotle, Archimedes, and other scholars he had heard about, and then he had their works translated into Arabic in the Bayt al-Hikma. Al-Mamun also founded an observatory and hospitals.

Islamic theology further stimulated Arab thinking. Arab intellectuals tried to integrate Islamic tradition with Greek philosophy. However, their acceptance of the ideas of Aristotle and Plato brought them into conflict with Islamic theolo-

This world map, which shows seven climatic zones, was drawn in Tunisia between 1099 and 1165 CE.

gians, who opposed such radical thinking in spite of the caliphs' well-established predisposition to the study of science.

Arab mathematicians, physicians, and philosophers played a major role in the introduction of ancient Greek knowledge to western Europe. Their translations into Latin of Arabic books based on ancient Greek sources were medieval Christendom's main source of information about the classical world.

Among the most celebrated Islamic scientist-philosophers of the period were Ibn Sina (Avicenna; 980–1037 CE) and Ibn Ruhd (Averroës; 1126–1198 CE). Born in Bukhara (a city in present-day Iran), Avicenna became a court physician by the age of 18. In his *Kitab ash-shifa* (Book of Healing), he treated a great number of subjects: logic, natural sciences, geometry, astronomy, arithmetic, and metaphysics. His work owes a great deal to Aristotle and to Neoplatonism, a school of Greek religious-mystical philosophy developed (notably by Plotinus) in the third century CE and based on the earlier writings of Plato. Avicenna also wrote *Al-Qanan fi at-tibb* (The Canon of Medicine), an encyclopedia, derived from Greek and Arab knowledge, that for centuries was a standard work in the universities of Europe. *Al-Qanan fi at-tibb* is widely regarded as the most celebrated book, eastern or western, in medical history.

The physician and judge Averroës was born in Córdoba. He, too, wrote a book on medicine, but the major body of his work dealt with the relation between religious law and philosophy. Because of his unorthodox thinking, he was considered a heretic by Christians and Muslims alike. He eventually became celebrated for his lengthy commentaries on the writings of Aristotle, which were translated into Latin in the 12th century CE and had an enormous influence on the development of philosophy in Europe.

AVICENNA
ex Codice antiqvo Galem.

Another important transmitter of ancient knowledge—in this case Indian mathematics—to western Europe was the Arab mathematician Mohammed ibn Musa al-Khwarizmi (c. 780–850 CE). Today, the familiar numbers 0 to 9 are known as Arabic numerals because, although they were developed in ancient India, they arrived in western Europe by way of Arab culture.

So-called Arabic numerals developed from Brahmi numerals, which were first used in Indian Buddhist inscriptions

This 17th-century-CE copper engraving depicts Ibn Sina (also known as Avicenna), one of the most celebrated Islamic scientist-philosophers.

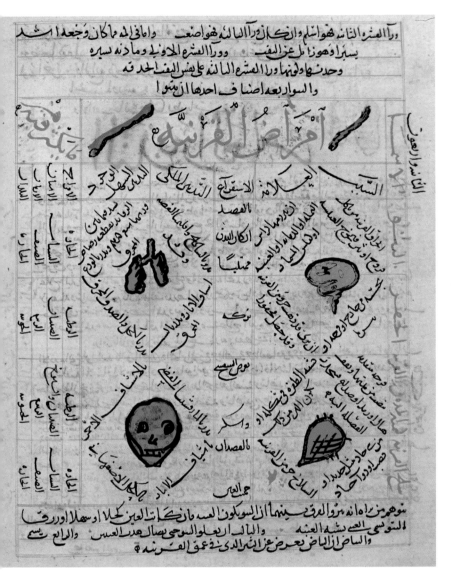

*This page is from a 14th-century-CE edition of **Al-Qanan fi at-tibb** by Ibn Sina.*

method of adding and subtracting became known as algorism, from *Algorismus*, which was the Latin rendition of the name Al-Khwarizmi. Born in Uzbekistan, Al-Khwarizmi spent the greater part of his life working in the Bayt al-Hikma in Baghdad. Al-Khwarizmi also wrote influential books on astrology and astronomy, and he re-worked *Geography*, a work by the first-century-CE Greek scientist Ptolemy.

Islamic economy

From its beginnings in the seventh century CE, the economy of Islam grew very quickly. Trade became increasingly international and money circulated throughout the empire. At one point, the trade in date fruit alone mobilized 100,000 camels, while melon and sugar-cane were almost equally important. Islamic trade reached its peak at the end of the eighth century CE. Two hundred years later, the first symptoms of its decline were visible. When the Arabs lost control of their empires, the era of their wealth was over and the Islamic world was put on the defensive.

While Christian merchants were still keeping their administrations in order with great difficulty, their Muslim counterparts were using "Indian" numbers to keep their accounts. The Arab credit industry was developing too. Merchants did not dare to travel with large amounts of money—there were far too many robbers laying in wait for them—and so preferred to make use of bills of exchange. The practice worked well and later became common in Christian Europe. In the Arab trade centers, people loaned and invested money, bought shares, and earned interest on investments. The money trade in cities such as Córdoba and Baghdad did not differ fundamentally from that in modern centers; most aspects of modern banking were present in a rudimentary form.

around 300 to 200 BCE. The earliest known document to use the numbers 0 to 9 and the system of decimal positional notation (in which 10 stands for one ten and zero units) is *The Parts of the Universe*, an Indian thesis on cosmology written in Sanskrit around 458 CE. The numbering system was first communicated to the Arabs by an Indian ambassador to the court of Al-Mansur. Around 825 CE, Al-Khwarizmi wrote *The Book of Adding and Subtracting by Indian Methods*, and it was through a 12th-century-CE translation of this work that the knowledge arrived in Europe. This

The rule of the caliphate

In the early years of the Umayyad dynasty, caliph Mu'awiyah and his successors struggled to impose central authority on many of their Arab subjects. The Bedouin were anything but servile; they were desert-dwellers who were accustomed to virtually unlimited freedom. Mu'awiyah often had to confer with his aids for hours to convince them of the validity and purpose of his proposed measures. Although Mu'awiyah's successors had greater authority, elements of that desert freedom continued to prevail. The Muslim army was notable for its fierce independence; soldiers could not be persuaded to give up their tribal loyalties, and army bases often looked more like civil war battlegrounds than bases for disciplined soldiery. Bloody conflicts took place in almost every garrison.

Under the Abbasid caliphate founded by Abu al-Abbas, the caliph became an absolute ruler. Abu al-Abbas, the ruthless "Bloodshedder" who massacred the Umayyad family, sent the Bedouin back to the desert and surrounded himself with subordinates from Byzantium and the Persian Empire. His new men brought with them a different attitude; they came from a tradition of respect for designated legal authority. Al-Mansur, who succeeded Abu al-Abbas as caliph and consolidated Abbasid power, was no less despotic. From his time onward, caliphs became almost completely isolated from their subjects. Amid the grand Persian ceremonies they introduced at court, the Abbasid caliphs lived in great luxury; the last traces of the simple desert lifestyle of a tribal sheikh disappeared from the imperial court.

The caliph existed in surroundings of fairy-tale opulence, learning only via his intermediaries what was happening outside the palace gates. Born in a closed harem, surrounded by women of many nationalities, and used to the atmosphere of intrigue at court, the caliph was preyed upon by sycophants and schemers. The word *Hajib*, which was used for the caliph's attendant or chamberlain, meant literally "curtain" or "screen"; the sensible caliph trusted no one and needed to be protected. Yet the caliphs were aware that they could not ignore the people altogether. To maintain their popularity, they employed court poets to create propaganda about the greatness of the caliphate. Al-Mansur, for example, was portrayed as a simple, pious Muslim who strove to protect the rights of the weaker members of society.

This earthenware bottle with a surface painting of four hares was made by Muslim artists in Granada, Spain, in the 10th century CE.

THE MOVE TO SAMARRA

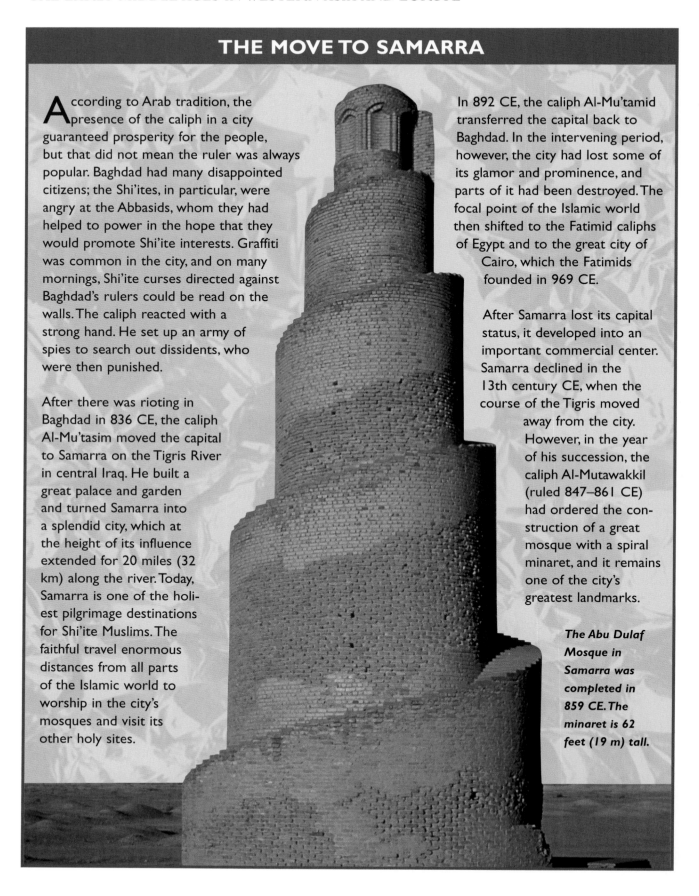

According to Arab tradition, the presence of the caliph in a city guaranteed prosperity for the people, but that did not mean the ruler was always popular. Baghdad had many disappointed citizens; the Shi'ites, in particular, were angry at the Abbasids, whom they had helped to power in the hope that they would promote Shi'ite interests. Graffiti was common in the city, and on many mornings, Shi'ite curses directed against Baghdad's rulers could be read on the walls. The caliph reacted with a strong hand. He set up an army of spies to search out dissidents, who were then punished.

After there was rioting in Baghdad in 836 CE, the caliph Al-Mu'tasim moved the capital to Samarra on the Tigris River in central Iraq. He built a great palace and garden and turned Samarra into a splendid city, which at the height of its influence extended for 20 miles (32 km) along the river. Today, Samarra is one of the holiest pilgrimage destinations for Shi'ite Muslims. The faithful travel enormous distances from all parts of the Islamic world to worship in the city's mosques and visit its other holy sites.

In 892 CE, the caliph Al-Mu'tamid transferred the capital back to Baghdad. In the intervening period, however, the city had lost some of its glamor and prominence, and parts of it had been destroyed. The focal point of the Islamic world then shifted to the Fatimid caliphs of Egypt and to the great city of Cairo, which the Fatimids founded in 969 CE.

After Samarra lost its capital status, it developed into an important commercial center. Samarra declined in the 13th century CE, when the course of the Tigris moved away from the city. However, in the year of his succession, the caliph Al-Mutawakkil (ruled 847–861 CE) had ordered the construction of a great mosque with a spiral minaret, and it remains one of the city's greatest landmarks.

The Abu Dulaf Mosque in Samarra was completed in 859 CE. The minaret is 62 feet (19 m) tall.

The splendor of Baghdad

Al-Mansur founded the city of Baghdad on the banks of the Tigris River around 762 CE. He laid out a circular complex that was essentially a palace and government center. It stood within triple concentric walls, contained four quarters, and was around 1.75 miles (2.7 km) in diameter. From the grand mosque and palace at its heart, four roads radiated outward. Outside the walls were residential and market areas. Transcending Damascus as a center of trade, craftsmanship, and culture, the new capital city became the commercial hub of the Islamic world. All its wealth was displayed in the streets, and craftsmen worked in the open air. Huge crowds congested the markets, buying, selling, and transporting a range of goods.

The caliph was afraid of riots and wanted to keep potentially volatile market crowds at a safe distance. He declared the downtown area of the city a sacred space and forbade anyone except himself from entering it on horseback. Some people disputed Al-Mansur's authority, and in later years, opposition to the caliphs increased to such a degree that, for a period in the ninth century CE, they were forced to move their capital to Samarra in central Iraq to escape rioting in Baghdad. Until that crisis, however, Baghdad was a city without equal in the world. Under Al-Mahdi (ruled 775–785 CE), Harun ar-Rashid (ruled 786–809 CE), and Al-Mamun (ruled 813–833 CE), Baghdad was the richest place on Earth, and merchant ships from Africa, China, and India docked on the city's wharves. Baghdad's greatness in these years is immortalized in the stories of *One Thousand and One Nights*.

See also:

The Caliphate (volume 6, page 764) •
Mohammed and Islam (volume 6, page 736) •
Rise of Islam (volume 6, page 752)

The Tigris River flows through the center of Baghdad, the modern capital of Iraq.

THE AGE OF CHARLEMAGNE

The Franks, who gave their name to modern-day France, rose to dominance from the fifth century CE onward. Some 300 years later, Charlemagne became ruler of the largest empire Europe had seen since the fall of ancient Rome.

Clovis I (ruled 481–511 CE) founded the line of Merovingian kings that ruled the Frankish kingdom in western Europe until 751 CE, when it was replaced by the Carolingian dynasty.

Clovis was not the first king of the Franks (in fact, a federation of various western Germanic tribes), but he greatly expanded the territory he inherited in central Europe. He built an empire that included all of the former Roman province of Gaul, except Burgundy and what is now Provence.

Originally a pagan, Clovis married a Catholic princess and converted to Catholic Christianity, rather than the Arian form common among the Franks and other Germanic groups. (Arian Christians, named for the fourth-century-CE churchman Arius of Alexandria, held that Christ was partly human rather than fully divine.) The name of the Merovingian dynasty comes from Merovech, Clovis's grandfather.

Following Clovis's death in Paris in 511 CE, his empire rapidly disintegrated as his sons squabbled over their inheritance. Frankish law insisted that any inheritance be divided between the sons of the deceased, even if the dead man was the king. Such a law invited problems for the Merovingian dynasty.

Ultimately, no individual Merovingian emerged from the disputes in full charge. In addition, during the century following Clovis's death, the divided imperial power faced an increasing challenge from the aristocracy. As the empire declined, the Frankish elite prospered, happy to accept gifts from the Merovingians for their support but paying less and less regard to their former rulers. The outposts of Clovis's empire fell first. Local nobles took power in Aquitaine, Bavaria, and Brittany. By the end of the sixth century CE, the united Frankish Empire had been replaced by a number of competing kingdoms.

Changing political power

As central political power declined in the former empire, so too did trade and the use of money. Each region and even each rural estate was forced to become self-sufficient, producing what its inhabitants needed. Increasingly, wealth was measured in land rather than money. The family with the most land could produce the most food and other resources and was therefore the richest and most powerful.

Large landowners did not work the land themselves. They leased the land to tenant farmers, dependents who worked the farms and gave the owners a share of

This reliquary depicting the emperor Charlemagne contains part of his skull. The bust was made in the 14th century CE.

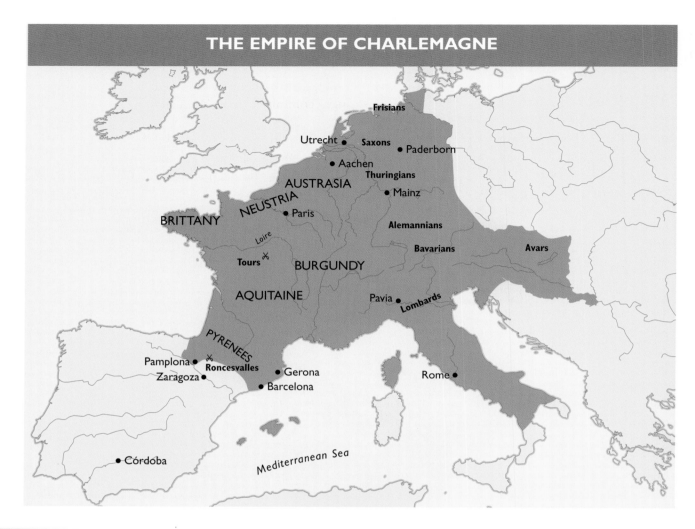

THE EMPIRE OF CHARLEMAGNE

KEY

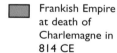
Frankish Empire at death of Charlemagne in 814 CE

✕ Major battle

the harvest in return for protection. This arrangement freed the landowners to spend their time on administrative tasks and leisure activities, such as hunting.

Under the Merovingians, the most important landowner remained the monarch. The king owned the largest rural estates, which were spread throughout his domain. His power rested on personal prestige as well as on wealth. He acquired that prestige in large part through lineage—his descent from the family of Clovis—but also through his reputation as an administrator. The king's subjects had two major expectations: that he should protect his people and expand the frontiers of their territories.

The other key landowner was the Roman Catholic Church. In effect, the church was integrated with the structures of political and social power. Leading positions in the church hierarchy were typically in the hands of members of either aristocratic or royal families.

As the Merovingian Empire fell apart and royal authority decreased, real power increasingly rested not with the king but with the aristocracy. In each of the new kingdoms that arose, the royal role in administration was gradually taken over by the *major palatii* (mayor of the palace). The Merovingian system had developed from one current in the Roman Empire, under which large landowners had appointed a *major domus* (supervisor of the household) to oversee several estates. The Merovingian mayors slowly gained more power, taking charge of personnel at court, advising the monarch on whom to appoint as counts, and finally becoming commanders of the royal army.

The rise of Pépin

By the mid-seventh century CE, the power of the Franks was restricted to the area north of the Loire River, where two Frankish kingdoms existed side by side: Neustria, in the northwest of Clovis's former empire, and Austrasia, in the northeast of his former lands. Each kingdom was run by a *major palatii* intent on subjugating the other. In 687 CE, Pépin, mayor of Austrasia, defeated his Neustrian counterpart at Testry. The victory brought both territories under Pépin's control, a blow to the authority of the Merovingian kings.

Pépin's mayoral dynasty then claimed a growing share of the former royal prerogatives of protection and expansion. The dynasty eventually came to be called the Carolingians after its most famous rulers, Charles Martel and Charlemagne (*Carolus* was Latin for "Charles"). Pépin attacked the Frisians in the territory north of Austrasia and, convincingly defeating their king, reoccupied the ancient Roman stronghold of Utrecht.

Pépin combined his territorial expansion with support for the church; missionaries entered the newly conquered areas to bring the Catholic god to the people. To some extent, Pépin acted out of religious conviction. However, he also recognized the political profit to be gained from his missionary activities. The conversion of his new subjects to Christianity would consolidate his con-

quest. Pépin used Anglo-Saxon rather than Frankish missionaries. The Anglo-Saxons had converted to Christianity earlier in the seventh century CE and were strongly committed to the conversion effort. In addition, Anglo-Saxon priests were the only ones in this period to recognize the spiritual authority of the pope in Rome. Their role proved highly significant in fostering the subsequent contact between the Carolingians and the pope. For its part, the church generally supported the mayors of the palace, such as Pépin, rather than the Merovin-

Clovis I, depicted in this engraving from the 17th century CE, was the founder of the Merovingian dynasty.

This Frankish coin was made in the sixth century CE.

Victory at Tours

Meanwhile, the Islamic Moors in Spain were also seeking new conquests. They had conquered almost the whole Iberian Peninsula in just five years after arriving from Africa in 711 CE; now, they were looking farther afield. Their cavalry periodically crossed the Pyrenees Mountains to raid Aquitaine. In 732 CE, a great Moorish army of cavalry swept onto the plains of Aquitaine. The Moors were able to defeat Duke Odo of Aquitaine decisively at the Battle of the River Garonne.

In response to a call for help from Odo, Charles led his army south to face the Muslim forces. Meeting the enemy near Tours, he ordered his cavalry to dismount and fight on foot alongside the infantry. The Muslim cavalry, faced with the great mass of infantry, could make no headway. They simply smashed themselves to pieces against the unmoving body of Frankish soldiers.

Although his footsoldiers defeated the Islamic horsemen, Martel was very impressed with the enemy cavalry and believed it was necessary to revise Frankish military strategy; the cavalry needed to become more important.

Martel's decision was not just a military one; it also had great economic and political significance. At the time, the Frankish cavalry was less important and much smaller than the infantry. Although every free man had the right to be a soldier in the service of his lord, only the richest members of society could afford the equipment and the horse necessary to serve in the cavalry. Martel saw that, in order to increase the number of cavalry, he would have to increase the number of wealthy landowners. In the name of the king, Martel seized land on a large scale from the church. He then granted it to his followers on condition that each new

gian kings, who no longer seemed able to provide protection.

Charles Martel

Pépin died in 714 CE, and power passed to his illegitimate son Charles. Charles continued the drive to reassert Frankish predominance. Rebel lords soon realized that Charles had impressive military abilities. His fighting skills earned him the nickname Martel (the Hammer). Charles defeated the Frisians in the Rhine Delta, after they had reclaimed the conquests of Pépin during the changeover of power. He followed in his father's footsteps by sending Anglo-Saxon missionaries to consolidate the conquest. He waged war on the Saxons, the Thuringians, the Alemannians, and the Bavarians, expanding the Frankish presence in the Germanic lands and ultimately uniting the realm under his authority.

estate owner swear allegiance to him. Under this system, each grant of land was called a fief or fiefdom.

This innovation greatly strengthened the position of the Carolingians. At a stroke, Martel augmented the old aristocracy with a group of newcomers who were entirely dependent upon him for their social position.

The foundations of feudalism

The battle-weary Martel died in his palace at Quierzy-sur-Oise in October of 741 CE. He had demonstrated that he was more than capable of carrying out the key tasks of a king, having both expanded the territories of the Franks and protected them from Muslim invasion. However, he had not claimed the royal title for himself or his family. Throughout his life, he had continued to serve as mayor, accepting the authority of the Merovingian dynasty.

Martel's victory at Tours was highly significant. It proved to be the last attempt at an Islamic invasion of western Europe, apart from the Iberian Peninsula. It has traditionally been cast by historians as the moment in which Christian culture was saved in Europe—then more generally referred to as Christendom—and the Muslims were prevented from spreading north throughout western Europe. Yet, in historical terms, Martel's chief importance is his introduction of the fiefdom. His policy of granting large estates in return for an oath of loyalty formed the basis of the feudal system that shaped European political organization in the centuries that followed. Indeed, it is from the Latin for fief, *feudum*, that the word *feudalism* derives.

These silver earrings were made by Frankish craftsmen in the sixth or seventh century CE.

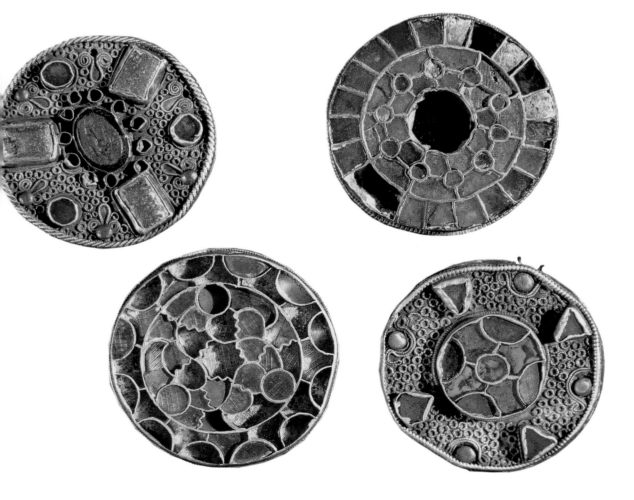

The first Carolingian king

On Martel's death, his state and authority were divided between his two sons, Pépin and Carloman, in accordance with Frankish law. At first, the two worked together. In 747 CE, however, Carloman passed his power to Pépin and withdrew to a monastery. Pépin promptly removed Carloman's sons from government, to the advantage of

Charles Martel, though never king, was effectively the ruler of the Franks. This illustration dates to the 19th century CE.

his own, and called the lords of the Frankish Empire together in council in 751 CE. They deposed the last of the Merovingian kings, Childeric III, and elected Pépin king.

Pépin set an important precedent by seeking a church blessing for his rule. Prior to his election as king, he wrote to Pope Zachary (ruled 741–752 CE) asking, according to one contemporary historian, "whether it was right that those who were of royal lineage and were called kings but had no power in their kingdoms should still be called kings." The pope replied in the negative, lending support to Pépin's revolution. Pépin was also anointed, or blessed, first by Saint Boniface and then in 754 CE by Zachary's successor, Pope Stephen II (ruled 752–757 CE). (Saint Boniface was an English nobleman, originally named Wynfrith, who became a Benedictine monk and led missions to pagan tribes in what is now Germany.)

Pépin, the first king of the great Carolingian line, could not claim royal blood. Instead, he compensated by having the blessing of the church and, by association, of God himself. Pépin also secured the pope's political backing. The arrangement had advantages for both sides; the pope needed allies against the political power of the Lombards.

Papacy under attack

The Lombards were a Germanic people who had invaded the Italian Peninsula in the sixth century CE. At the time, the nominal power in the region was the Byzantine Empire, but the Byzantine rulers, who had their hands full with the Arabs in western Asia, largely ignored Rome and their other Italian possessions. After 568 CE, the Lombards established a kingdom centered on Pavia and then expanded south. The papacy also benefited from the lack of Byzantine control by

taking over the administration of the area around Rome.

By the eighth century CE, the papal territory had come under severe pressure from the Lombards. Pope Zachary knew that he could not expect help from the Byzantine Empire; its own capital at Constantinople was under siege. Instead, the pope looked to the mayor of the Franks for support.

In return for anointing Pépin I as king, the pope—by now Stephen II had come to the papal throne—got military help in Italy from Pépin's army. Pépin defeated the Lombards and passed their lands to the papacy. Pépin was then anointed with both his sons, Carloman and Charlemagne. The papacy had in effect offered its blessing not just to a king but to a new royal dynasty.

Some historians have argued that, by accepting the blessing of the pope, Pépin made his kingship dependent on papal approval. Others, however, argue that Pépin owed the throne only to his own prestige and the support the new aristocrats of the fiefdoms pledged to him. The key to his elevation to the monarchy was his election by the council of lords rather than the blessing of the pope. Either way, it is certain that anointment by the pope increased the status of the new monarchy. Later Carolingian propaganda would compare the rulers of this dynasty to the Old Testament kings Saul and David.

The rise of Charlemagne

For the remainder of his reign, Pépin concentrated on consolidating his own position within the empire. On his death

This 19th-century-CE engraving depicts Charles Martel's victory over Muslim forces at the Battle of Tours.

in 768 CE, his sons, Carloman and Charlemagne, became rivals for the throne. Charlemagne made an alliance against his brother with his cousin, Duke Tassilo III of Bavaria. With the encouragement of his mother, he entered another alliance by marrying the daughter of the Lombard king Desiderius. The marriage drew condemnation from Pope

This modern illustration depicts Charlemagne as the ruler of both Europe and the church.

Stephen III (ruled 768–772 CE), who saw the alliance as a threat to his power. He denounced the marriage as "the work of the devil, an utterly illegal union, something insane, through which the superior Frankish blood would be polluted by the stinking faithless race of the Lombards from which, as everyone knew, the race of lepers was descended." No one is sure whether the pope's outburst had a direct effect, but Charlemagne did send his new bride back to the Lombards.

When Carloman died suddenly in 771 CE, Charlemagne declared himself sole king. Carloman's widow fled with her children to Desiderius, who cut off ties with Charlemagne and asked the new pope, Adrian I (ruled 772–795 CE) to anoint the sons of Carloman as kings. This forced Charlemagne's hand. He crossed the Alps and besieged and defeated the Lombards in their capital, Pavia. During the siege, his potential rivals, his nephews, disappeared.

At Easter in 774 CE, before the siege of Pavia was over, Charlemagne traveled to Rome. There, he celebrated the chief Christian festival in Saint Peter's Basilica and promised that he would restore to the pope his ancient rights and worldly territory. Once he had defeated the Lombards, Charlemagne deposed Desiderius and proclaimed himself the new ruler of the Lombards. He appointed Frankish lords to keep his new subjects obedient. Despite his promise, he added little to papal territory.

Onslaught against the Saxons

Charlemagne could now turn to other conquests. In 772 CE, he had had his first clash with the Saxons, a rival confederation of German tribes. The Saxons were pagans renowned for their fierce independence. Throughout their history, they had never submitted to the authority of a ruler. They were freemen who defended the independence of their villages, uniting in federation only in the face of great dangers. Charlemagne now set out to bring them within the bounds of his Christian kingdom.

The Saxons were formidable opponents, and Charlemagne's war against them lasted more than 30 years. He led no fewer than 18 campaigns against the Saxons. They in turn were coordinated by the warrior Widukind, who made successful use of guerrilla warfare in the great forests of Europe. The Franks had no real answer to the strategy, and they often resorted to massacring whatever Saxons they found.

Between 775 and 777 CE, Charlemagne mounted a series of campaigns that resulted in the enforced baptism of Saxons, who also agreed a treaty of allegiance to the Franks at a diet (convention) in Paderborn. When the Saxons rose again in opposition only a few years later, Charlemagne responded in 782 CE with the execution of 4,500 Saxons. Saxon exhaustion ended the long conflict in 804 CE. Charlemagne then resettled much of the Saxon population in Frankish or Frisian areas to break any final resistance and sent loyal Franks to occupy former Saxon territory.

The Germanic tribes

Charlemagne suppressed the freedom of all the Germanic tribes in a series of prolonged struggles similar to the one with the Saxons. The Bavarians and the Frisians, like the Saxons, refused to give up their traditional freedoms, as had been suggested in 754 CE by the murder of the missionary Saint Boniface in Frisian territory. Charlemagne repeatedly had to return to recently conquered areas, because the allies he had acquired among the Germanic tribes frequently turned out to be untrustworthy.

This gold talisman was found in Charlemagne's tomb at Aachen.

Finally, in 788 CE, with the deposing of his cousin and former ally Duke Tassilo III of Bavaria, Charlemagne ended any suggestion of Bavarian independence. He incorporated the Christian Bavarians into the empire together with the Alemannians and the Thuringians. The victory, and the end of the conflict with the Saxons, confirmed that Charlemagne had broken the power of the Germanic tribes. Even after the death of Charlemagne, his successors in the Carolingian dynasty had no need to fear revolts in this area.

To the east, in modern-day Hungary and Austria, Slavic peoples had founded principalities under the hegemony of the militarily powerful Avars. Charlemagne now unleashed the full might of the Frankish military machine against them, destroying the Avar kingdom so completely that the Avars as a people disappeared from history. Having removed the threat, Charlemagne made no attempt to subjugate their lands. He forced the Slavic principalities on his eastern borders to pay tribute to him but did not convert them to Christianity.

A celebrated defeat in Spain

At the diet of Paderborn in 777 CE, Charlemagne had accepted the submission of the Saxons, but he had also

This 16th-century-CE illustration depicts Stephen III, who became pope in 768 CE.

STEPHANVS · III · P · M ·

received a deputation from Spain. The Muslim lords of Barcelona, Gerona, and Huesca were seeking military help against Abd ar-Rahman, the Umayyad ruler of Córdoba. Abd ar-Rahman had escaped the slaughter of his clan by the Abassids (the ruling Muslim dynasty in the Middle East). Charlemagne saw an opportunity for glory and a chance to extend Christian territory. In 778 CE, he led an army across the Pyrenees and besieged Zaragoza. However, when the city proved harder to overcome than he had expected, he decided to retreat. On his way home, he attacked and devastated the Basque city of Pamplona.

As the retreating army crossed the Pyrenees, its rearguard was attacked in a narrow pass named Roncesvalles. The clash left many of Charlemagne's nobles dead, including Hroudland or Roland—described by Einhard (c. 770–840 CE), who wrote a life of Charlemagne, as warden of the Breton Marches (the territories on the border with Brittany). The warden's death is the subject of the renowned 11th-century-CE epic poem *La Chanson de Roland* (The Song of Roland).

In the poem (see box, page 801), the battle at Roncesvalles involves a mighty troop of Saracen knights. In reality, it was probably an ambush by Basques (perhaps in association with Muslim cavalry) seeking revenge for the attack on Pamplona. The earliest accounts of the battle suggest that the attack did indeed come from the Basques but that it was a minor skirmish.

Many historians argue, however, that a battle that assumed such importance in popular legend must have been far more significant at the time. As evidence, they point to the fact that, when he got back to Aquitaine, Charlemagne began reinforcing his defensive positions there. The historians argue that this suggests that Charlemagne had suffered a signifi-

CHARLEMAGNE'S ARMY

Charlemagne is often celebrated as a forerunner of the medieval knights, the nobles who competed in tournaments, fought in the crusades, and followed a code of honorable behavior known as chivalry. In medieval poems and romances, Charlemagne appeared as the ideal of chivalry.

Charlemagne fought 53 military campaigns and revolutionized the armies of Europe. With his fellow Frankish kings, he was a pioneer of the use of heavy cavalry in battle. His remarkable success was due to his effective use of mounted warriors, his careful military organization, and his ability to control very large armies. Scholars estimate that the king had as many as 35,000 well-equipped knights. An imperial edict of 792 CE required knights to fit themselves out with lances, shields, and long and short swords, as well as a horse. In 802 CE, the emperor decreed that knights should also have body armor, which at the time consisted of leather jerkins with small plates sewn on. In 805 CE, he ordered his knights to have a byrnie or tunic of chain mail. Knights also had to bring three months' worth of food when they gathered for service. Charlemagne usually gathered his army at Easter and campaigned during the summer. For smaller encounters, he used groups called *scarae*, a few hundred knights probably from his royal escort. Discipline was strict. Charlemagne forbade drunkenness and imposed heavy fines on those who failed to turn up for military service or who came without the required equipment. Desertion was punishable by execution and the confiscation of property.

This illustration from the 19th century CE depicts a Carolingian warrior.

cant setback in the mountains and expected more trouble. Some contend that Charlemagne was indeed attacked by a significant force of Islamic troops and suffered a serious defeat.

The making of an emperor

At the close of the eighth century CE, Charlemagne controlled most of western Europe. He was effectively the ruler of western Christendom, and contemporaries likened his empire to the ancient Roman Empire. By this time, the office of Roman emperor had acquired a sacred character. Following the conversion of Emperor Constantine to Christianity in the fourth century CE, the emperor was considered the head of all Christians and the protector of all believers.

Over the centuries after the fall of the Roman Empire in the west, the successor to the Roman emperors had been the ruler of the Byzantine or eastern Roman Empire in Constantinople. The Byzantine

emperor Leo III (ruled 717–741 CE), founder of the Isaurian dynasty, was a controversial figure who had banned the use of icons in Christian worship and come into open conflict with popes Gregory II (ruled 715–731 CE) and Gregory III (ruled 731–741 CE). In Rome, the papacy challenged the emperor's right to authority. Although the popes were nominally subjects of the eastern Roman Empire, they had moved to separate themselves from it politically by making alliances with the kings of the Franks and establishing an autonomous region around Rome and Ravenna. The Byzantine authorities allowed this Roman autonomy, asserting their influence only on Sicily and in southern Italy.

In the late eighth century CE, however, a document appeared that seemed to legitimize papal independence. Known as the Donatio Constantini (The Donation of Constantine), the purported Byzantine legal document recorded Constantine's

THE SONG OF ROLAND

The Song of Roland is the oldest known *chanson de geste* (song of heroic deeds), a type of epic poem that celebrated the achievements of Charlemagne and his knights. The poem was probably composed in the second half of the 11th century CE. *The Song of Roland* and other *chansons de geste* portray knights defending Christendom against Muslim soldiers, often called Saracens (from *sharqiyin*, Arabic for "easterners"). These poems were the earliest form of the literature of chivalry, a vast body of literature spanning the period from the 11th to the 16th century CE that honored knights, ladies, quests, and battles.

The poem transforms the facts of Charlemagne's ill-fated invasion of northern Spain in 778 CE into the stirring stuff of legend. In *The Song of Roland*, Charlemagne (who was 36 in 778 CE) is said to be 200 years old and his brief invasion of Spain becomes a seven-year campaign. Roland, said in the poem to be the nephew of Charlemagne, is a great warrior armed with a magnificent sword named Durandel. The poem recounts how, as the army passes through the narrow Pass of Roncesvalles in the Pyrenees, it is forced into a long line. Charlemagne in the vanguard gets farther and farther ahead of Roland in the rear.

Charlemagne has ordered Roland to blow his horn to summon help if he is in trouble, but when the rear is ambushed and under savage attack, Roland is reluctant to delay the king or put him in danger and does not raise the alarm. Only when the entire rear guard is wiped out and Roland, badly wounded, is alone does he blow the horn; in his last moments, he lays himself down on top of his sword to prevent it falling into enemy hands. Charlemagne rushes to the rescue, only to find the lifeless body of his beloved knight and loyal vassal.

This illustration from the 20th century CE depicts the ambush of Roland by Muslims at Roncesvalles.

Charlemagne is crowned emperor by Pope Leo III. This manuscript illustration was produced around 1450 CE.

granting of the western part of his empire to the pope in Rome. It is now known that the document was a forgery, probably created in the time of Pope Adrian, but it had a powerful effect at the time. It continued to play an important role in the Middle Ages, when the papacy used it to justify its claim to authority over the monarchs of Europe.

The emperor and the papacy

Charlemagne initially set out to maintain good relations with both Rome and Constantinople. He visited Rome again in 781 CE, to have his sons, Pépin and Louis, anointed as kings of the Lombards and of the Aquitanians respectively. He also recognized the Byzantine empress Irene as ruler. However, this cordial understanding ended abruptly in 787 CE, when Charlemagne led an assault on Byzantine-held southern Italy.

In May of 799 CE, local lords took Pope Leo III (ruled 795–816 CE) hostage. Leo escaped and fled across the Alps to take refuge with Charlemagne. The emperor's men escorted Leo safely back to Rome. When Charlemagne himself then traveled to Rome in November of 800 CE, Leo came to meet him as a mark of honor. The pope traveled not just 2 miles (3.2 km) outside Rome to greet the visitor, as was customary, but the full 12 miles (19 km) laid down in protocol for the reception of an emperor. Before a tribunal in Charlemagne's presence, Leo was cleared of all charges leveled by his enemies.

On Christmas Day, Charlemagne attended the mass celebrated by Leo in St. Peter's Basilica. Like his father before him, Charlemagne held the title *Patricius Romanorum* (Protector of the Romans). Leo now also crowned him *Imperator*

Augustus (August Emperor), emperor of the Roman Empire in the west. Charlemagne accepted the title but is said to have expressed surprise. His biographer Einhard quotes the king as saying that he would not have set foot in the basilica had he known of the planned coronation—yet the event had been arranged in advance. One interpretation of Einhard's story is that the new emperor was expressing humility; another is that he was irritated at being crowned apparently on the initiative of the pope.

Byzantium reacted angrily. In the eyes of the Byzantine emperor, Charlemagne was a usurper. Charlemagne seized Byzantine territory in Venice and threatened a large-scale invasion of Byzantine territory in southern Italy. It was only in 811 CE, 11 years after his coronation, that he was recognized as emperor by the Byzantine ruler Michael I, although not as emperor of the Romans.

Charlemagne's last years

After becoming emperor, Charlemagne largely withdrew from military campaigning, leaving the rigors of the battlefield to his subordinates. In the last years of his life, according to Einhard, he was racked by various sicknesses and ailments, possibly including gout.

In 806 CE, Charlemagne began to prepare for the succession, planning to divide the empire among his three sons. However, by 813 CE, the older two sons had died, making the succession straightforward. Charlemagne's remaining son, Louis, had been king of Aquitaine since 781 CE.

In 813 CE, Charlemagne himself crowned Louis co-emperor and designated him as his sole successor. He did not invite the pope to participate in the ceremony because he was eager to emphasize his own status and the independence of the imperial crown from the papacy. Charlemagne believed that no one but God had more authority than he did, and for years, he had included in all new laws the motto *Imperator a Deo Coronatus* (Emperor Crowned by God). Despite Charlemagne's view, however, the papacy retained the right to crown the emperor for another 700 years.

In 814 CE, Charlemagne died. The imperial chronicles recorded the event: "Emperor Charlemagne left this earth when he spent the winter at Aachen, more than 71 years old in the 47th year of his reign, the 43rd year since the conquest of Italy, and the 14th since he had been declared Emperor and Augustus, on the 28th of January."

See also:

The Carolingian Empire (volume 6, page 804) • Feudal Europe (volume 6, page 814)

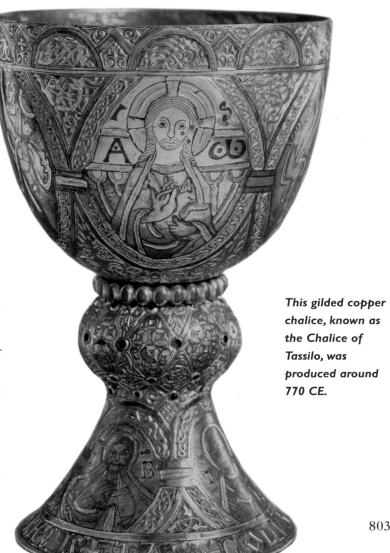

This gilded copper chalice, known as the Chalice of Tassilo, was produced around 770 CE.

THE CAROLINGIAN EMPIRE

Over the course of his long reign, the Frankish king Charlemagne took considerable steps to bind his territory together. After his death, however, the empire was torn apart by struggles among his son and grandsons.

Between 768 and 814 CE, the Frankish king Charlemagne created a huge empire that stretched over much of western and central Europe. He recognized that this great empire could not be maintained only by the sword or administrative control. Instead, it needed an active culture to hold it together. Charlemagne set out to create an *Imperium Christianum* (Empire of Christians) and to establish his court as the leading force in western Christendom in matters of education, culture, and religion, as well as the base for administration and justice.

The need for education was severe. Most of Charlemagne's subjects, including the aristocracy, were illiterate. During the turbulent centuries after the fall of the western Roman Empire, there had been little interest—outside the church—in scholarship and culture; education, always poor in terms of distribution and scale, had retreated behind the walls of monasteries.

The first efforts at remedying the situation had been made by Charlemagne's grandfather Charles Martel, who imported English monks to educate diplomats and staff in the court chancellery. Charlemagne followed his example, bringing together intellectuals from within the empire and abroad to educate members of the court. He required his family and the lay people of his entourage to study languages, history, and theology. Charlemagne himself learned Latin and Greek and studied astronomy and mathematics; he also set up a court library stocked with works of theology and literature.

Alcuin's educational reforms

A key figure in implementing Charlemagne's cultural and educational reforms was the Anglo-Saxon monk Alcuin. He was a pupil, teacher, and finally headmaster at the Cathedral School of York, one of the most celebrated educational establishments of its day. Then, from 782 CE onward, Alcuin taught at the Palatine school within Charlemagne's court at Aachen (see box, page 807). He reorganized the school and the whole educational establishment in the empire.

Alcuin was not opposed to the existing church schools but to the content of their curriculum, which was designed to train young men for the priesthood and was limited to reading and writing, with a little Latin and some psalm-singing. Alcuin introduced the study of the seven liberal arts (once approved for students in ancient Rome), which had been taught in England for

This ninth-century-CE manuscript illustration depicts Lothair I, son of Louis the Pious. The two spent many years in conflict.

This 18th-century-CE engraving depicts Charlemagne with the monk Alcuin, who did much to advance education at the emperor's court.

200 years. These subjects were music, astronomy, geometry, logic, arithmetic, grammar, and rhetoric. Together, study in these arts provided an education in all areas covered by western scholarship. Alcuin also put great emphasis on the study of Latin. In his celebrated *Epistula de litteris colendis* (Letter on the necessity of learning letters), written under Charlemagne's name, Alcuin argued that it was essential to use the correct language to study Christianity in order to avoid misunderstanding the scriptures.

Alcuin greatly broadened the education of the clergy and through them improved the level of popular education. In 796 CE, he became abbot of the Abbey of St. Martin at Tours. Alcuin's work there involved writing illustrated manuscripts with monks. His labors resulted in the development of a new simplified and more easily legible form of writing—the Carolingian minuscule script. This style of writing is the forerunner of modern Roman typefaces.

The Carolingian Renaissance

Alcuin worked alongside other leading intellectuals of his day at Charlemagne's court. The emperor supported Alcuin and his colleagues wherever possible and enjoyed conversing with the circle of learned men at his court; he seems to have felt at home in their company.

Einhard, a monk celebrated for his biography of Charlemagne, was originally a pupil of Alcuin. Befriended by his teacher, Einhard rose to prominence and was appointed superintendant of public buildings by Charlemagne. Einhard was a major figure at court. He later served as tutor to the emperor's grandson Lothair and was rewarded with large estates. Einhard's *Life of Charlemagne* (c. 833 CE) is more a study of the emperor's character than a work of historical narrative. Einhard heaps lavish praise on his patron.

Historians refer to the revival of culture and education that resulted from Charlemagne's efforts as the Carolingian Renaissance. The period is seen as a renaissance or rebirth because it followed the prolonged "dark age" (when learning and writing were not valued) that followed the collapse of the Roman Empire in the west. Alcuin is generally seen as the leading scholar of the Carolingian Renaissance. In addition to his educational reforms, he made changes to the liturgy of the Roman Catholic Church. In particular, he introduced the custom of singing the creed during mass. Alcuin wrote a good number of poems and composed 300 letters that are an invaluable source of information about Charlemagne's court.

The Carolingian Renaissance only lasted for one generation after the death of Charlemagne, but it had a profound effect on the course of European history. From a battered and disparate collection of peoples, a common culture evolved within a single political and religious institution. The culture's dominant actor, Charlemagne, was seen as the model Christian emperor.

Government of the empire

Each year, Charlemagne held a general assembly, either in core Frankish territory or in one of the regions he had conquered. The imperial court—which comprised his family, clergy, temporal officials, and educators—was joined by magistrates and nobles from all over the empire to hand down justice and to review all matters of importance, military and ecclesiastical as well as legal.

The marble throne of Charlemagne is in the Palatine Chapel in Aachen Cathedral in Aachen, Germany.

AACHEN AND THE PALATINE CHAPEL

At the beginning of his reign, Charlemagne had no single official permanent residence. Like previous Frankish kings, he would travel from one palace to another (depending on the season), taking his court with him and making necessary political and legal decisions as he went. In 794 CE, however, he decided to make Aachen a permanent base for his rule. He built a magnificent church there, the Palatine Chapel, which is today part of Aachen Cathedral.

The Palatine Chapel was consecrated in 805 CE. Its designer, Odo of Metz, based it on the Byzantine Church of San Vitale in Ravenna. The chapel's central area, domed and in the shape of an octagon, stands within a two-story ambulatory with 16 sides. Above the dome, the cupola is 102 feet (30.9 m) high. The Charlemagne Shrine in the choir holds the emperor's remains. The chapel also contains a marble throne believed to have been made in Charlemagne's era and said to have been used for the coronations of a total of 32 emperors between 936 and 1531 CE.

One of Charlemagne's most difficult problems was how to deal with the aristocracy, who were an essential component of these assemblies. Crucial to Charlemagne's relationship with them was the oath of allegiance.

Frankish lords were not subordinate to the kingdom, the empire, or the state, but to the individual person of the king, to whom they took a personal oath of loyalty. The oath was rooted in ancient Germanic traditions—in particular in the concept of *comitatus* (companionship) described by the Roman author Tacitus in his first-century-CE treatise *De Germania*, which recorded the customs of the Germanic peoples. According to Tacitus, a Germanic leader of the first century CE had a group of crack troops called his companionship, whose members had sworn their allegiance to him. When the leader appeared on the battlefield, he would be surrounded by these troops, who would consider it the greatest honor to die for him.

This concept appeared in several Germanic societies. The Merovingian kings had a form of *comitatus*. At their court, a group of warriors known as a *trustis* protected the king's person and property. Its members (called *antrustions*) were bound to their lord by a personal oath. At the time of the Roman Empire, lords in Gaul and Spain also had warrior bands bound to their service, but by a slightly different system; the lord offered protection as a patron and modest remuneration, while warriors provided military service in return.

Under the Carolingian kings, institutions resembling the *comitatus* merged with those of the Roman estates. A subservient class of *vassi* (vassals) emerged. They supplied military, administrative, or judicial services or labor to the lord, while the lord provided protection and maintained his vassals. The relationship was formalized in the vassals' oath of allegiance. Once entered into, vassalage was lifelong. The ceremony for the swearing of the vassalage oath was called commendation. The vassal kneeled before the lord, placed his hands in those of the lord, and swore allegiance. The lord then raised the vassal up and kissed him. The lord provided the vassal with gifts— sometimes horses, food, or fighting equipment, but primarily land. From the time of Charles Martel, land took the form of the fiefdoms.

Imperial administration

For administrative purposes, the Frankish Empire was divided into local districts, each called a *pagus* or *gau*. The local governor was called a *comes* or count. As a

THE VIKING THREAT

By the mid-ninth century CE, when the Carolingian Empire was being divided on the death of Louis the Pious, the Vikings had already been appearing on Frankish coasts for a century, initially as traders but subsequently as violent raiders. These northern warriors from what is now Denmark, Sweden, and Norway were members of closely related clans of north Germanic origin who had settled in Scandinavia.

At the time, the Vikings' home territory was hardly known to the peoples of Charlemagne's empire—beyond tales of a vast northern land with savage inhabitants suffering in biting cold. The Vikings were pagans who for centuries had battled one another for territory, partly because of their customs of inheritance, which—in contrast to those of the Franks—required that all land be left to the oldest son. The younger sons got nothing and had to find a new piece of land. After centuries, most of the land was taken. With insufficient territory and agricultural techniques that were too primitive to feed a growing population, the Vikings faced a crisis.

A class of landless warriors emerged with nowhere to go at a time when powerful chieftains were establishing Scandinavian monarchies. Under these kings, plundering was accepted and even applauded, but it was not permitted within the kingdom, so the landless sons had to travel abroad in search of land and wealth. The more enterprising of them took to the sea.

Charlemagne, recognizing the threat at least in part, had stationed fleets along the coasts for protection, but his grandsons paid no heed to the increasing Viking threat. The Vikings pillaged well

The Vikings attacked the coastal settlements of the Carolingian Empire in longships such as this. In the ninth century CE, they sacked Frankish cities located on the banks of the Seine and Loire rivers.

within the empire, following rivers such as the Seine, the Loire, and the Somme to attack Frankish cities.

The raiders gained a reputation for invincibility, and no one in imperial authority dared to take serious action against them. By the close of the ninth century CE, individual counts were able to gain immense prestige by organizing resistance to the raiders in their regions. Men such as Baldwin Iron-Arm, defender of Flanders, proved with every victory that imperial power had failed and that only the local counts could provide effective resistance.

For all their violence and persistence, the Vikings gained no permanent possessions in the Carolingian Empire except in the lower Seine Valley. After their settlement in this region around 900 CE, the local Vikings became known as Normans (men from the north) and the region became Normandy.

This ninth-century-CE bronze statue depicts the emperor Charlemagne.

result of Charlemagne's conquests, the number of *gaus* increased considerably, reaching well over 200. Central control was virtually impossible; communication between regions was extremely limited, and administrators were generally illiterate. Therefore, the counts ran their *gaus* quite independently.

Charlemagne looked for ways to maintain his control within these limitations. He appointed trusted subordinates as counts and required them to swear the same oath of allegiance that was used for fiefdoms. He began to require sitting counts to swear allegiance as well. Aristocrats had to reaffirm their subordination to the king in order to be allowed to rule small provinces.

Charlemagne kept a tight rein on his counts, requiring administrative reports from them. He traveled extensively throughout the empire and sent trusted envoys called *missi dominici* (the lord's messengers) to observe government in the *gaus*. The messengers usually traveled in pairs consisting of a clerical official and a civil servant. Counts had to be ready for surprise visits from the *missi*. The emperor did not hesitate to depose any count judged to be guilty of bad administration.

Charlemagne also issued imperial orders called capitularies. Originally, these orders were oral, but they began to be recorded in writing toward the end of Charlemagne's reign. Among them were orders to take the oath of allegiance or to teach all Christians to say the Lord's Prayer. However, Charlemagne respected and recorded the traditions of many of the tribal peoples in his empire. Some of the emperor's most important capitularies were served as addenda to tribal regulations.

ICONOCLASM

In the eighth and ninth centuries CE, the Christian world was divided by a major international controversy over iconoclasm (from the Greek words *eikon*, meaning "image," and *klaien*, meaning "break"), the denunciation and banning of religious images in worship. The use of religious images had become common in the eastern part of the Roman Empire. Some opponents likened it to the worship of idols, forbidden in the Ten Commandments. Some supporters were probably influenced by their opposition to Islam, which bans pictorial images in places of worship.

The Byzantine emperor Leo III denounced the use of icons in 726 CE and banned it four years later. Many Christians in western Europe denounced him as a heretic and enemy of the faith, and he was condemned by the pope. The stakes were raised even higher under Leo's successor, Constantine V; people using images in worship were persecuted, and the use of images was condemned as idolatry at a church council in Hiera. Later in the century, policy changed in Constantinople when the empress Irene called the Seventh Council of Nicaea in 787 CE. Iconoclasm was denounced, and the religious use of images was reinstated.

Charlemagne (or those writing in his name) addressed the subject around 791 CE in the *Libri Carolini* (Caroline Books). The work objected to the decision reached at Nicaea yet, at the same time, rebuked iconoclasts for faithlessness. Iconoclasm came back into vogue in the east in the ninth century CE, but the veneration of icons was finally restored in 842 CE at the Council of Orthodoxy.

Given the limited means available, Charlemagne's method created something close to a guarantee of proper government across his vast empire. Yet regional diversity, regardless of the imperial attitude to it, meant that the empire remained difficult to control. The empire was not a natural unit; it was an assembly of core and conquered territories that were peopled by a mixture of tribes.

The empire after Charlemagne

As Charlemagne's reign drew to a close, his great European empire faced a difficult future. The granting of fiefdoms and the oath of allegiance bound subjects to the crown, but the system needed regular supplies of new land. Because new territories offered the promise of new landholdings for individual lords, it depended on the king making repeated conquests. This promise was already fading by the time Charlemagne was made emperor in 800 CE; he had expanded the empire as far as he could. The nobility within his domain had to live off their existing estates.

On his accession in 814 CE, Charlemagne's son Louis the Pious had to prove himself to both a power-hungry aristocracy and a domineering pope, Leo III. Louis also had to deal with the Vikings, who were already menacing the coasts. Despite all the work of Carolingians in the sphere of education and the administrative structure imposed by Charlemagne, the empire Louis inherited was far from unified in the *gaus*, where the ruling counts wanted to free themselves from imperial control. The minting of coins, the administration of justice, and the collection of tolls had been the prerogative of the king or emperor since the time of the early Merovingian kings, but now the counts wanted to make themselves masters of these lucrative royal rights. However, Louis's biggest challenge came from his own family.

A struggle among brothers

Almost as soon as Louis was installed as emperor, the question of who would succeed him presented itself. He had three sons: Lothair, another Louis, and Pépin. In 817 CE, Louis laid down plans for the succession in a decree called the *Ordinatio imperii*. Lothair was made co-emperor, while the younger sons, Louis and Pépin, were given the kingdoms of Bavaria and Aquitaine, respectively. Because of this division, Louis and Pépin became known as Louis the German and Pépin of Aquitaine. In 823 CE, however, Louis the Pious had a fourth son, Charles (later called Charles the Bald), who was born to Louis's second wife, Judith.

Louis's earlier decree stood in contravention of Frankish law, which required the equal division of a legacy among all legitimate sons. Judith worked hard to promote the interests of her own son, Charles the Bald, provoking the opposition of her stepsons. In 830 CE, the older sons rebelled against Louis and Judith. The emperor himself was captured by Pépin. However, the emperor's supporters fostered dissension among the rebels. Pépin and Louis the German rebelled against their brother Lothair and realigned themselves with their father, who was restored to power by October of the same year.

Louis the Pious then introduced a new scheme for the inheritance, the *Divisio regnorum*, under which the empire would be divided into four equal kingdoms that would become independent when he died. The brothers rebelled again in 833 CE, with the support of Pope Gregory IV and leading churchmen, and Louis was forced to abdicate. Lothair was briefly emperor, but the following year, as the brothers continued to fight among themselves, Louis was restored to power once more.

Conflicts over the succession continued. When Pépin died in 838 CE, Louis gave his kingdom of Aquitaine to Charles the Bald against the protests of Pépin's sons, who rose up in revolt. The rebellion was put down, and the emperor once again divided his empire, this time between Lothair, Charles, and Louis the German. Lothair, as the eldest son, was entitled to the one thing that could not be divided: the emperor's crown. Charles the Bald and Louis the German were prepared to recognize his sovereignty for the sake of appearances—but no more than that. All three brothers tried to gain support among the counts through extensive gift-giving in

Louis the German, a son of Louis the Pious, became king of the eastern Frankish kingdom after the Treaty of Verdun in 843 CE.

This ninth-century-CE manuscript illustration depicts Charles the Bald surrounded by various courtiers and churchmen.

the *gaus*. The counts profited greatly from the conflict.

Dissolution of an empire

The death of Louis the Pious in 840 CE was a catalyst for further conflict, and within three years, the empire had split. As eldest son, Lothair claimed control of the empire. However, in 841 CE, he was defeated at the Battle of Fontenay by the troops of Charles the Bald and Louis the German. The three brothers divided the legacy in the Treaty of Verdun in 843 CE. Louis the German received Francia Orientalis (the eastern Frankish kingdom), while Charles the Bald was given Francia Occidentalis (the western kingdom); these territories would become modern Germany and France, respectively. Lothair kept the title of emperor and was given the central imperial territories, known as Francia Media, stretching from Friesland down to and including Rome, with parts of Italy, Alsace, and Burgundy.

Lothair's empire did not last. It was divided among his sons after his death, so a line of weak buffer states emerged between the territories of Charles and Louis. In 870 CE, the two kings divided the northern part of Lothair's legacy, following the death of his oldest son who had ruled it. The remainder of the former emperor's domain fell into the hands of a series of adventurers; his crown was claimed by various kings.

Charles the Bald, who had to defend his western realm against both the coastal attacks of the Vikings and the land attacks of Louis the German, decided to engage the powerful magnates of his realm in its defense. Allotting them huge tracts of land to defend, Charles thereby established the subsequent feudal territories of France.

See also:

The Age of Charlemagne (volume 6, page 788) • Feudal Europe (volume 6, page 814) • The Holy Roman Empire (volume 6, page 832)

FEUDAL EUROPE

In the centuries immediately following the reign of Charlemagne, the power of the Frankish kings lessened, while that of the regional lords increased. During this period, a social structure known as feudalism developed.

By 877 CE, when Charles the Bald's death brought an end to his reign as king of the western Frankish kingdom, the great European empire created by his grandfather Charlemagne had descended into chaos. The united Christian realm of which Charlemagne had dreamed had degenerated into a collection of autonomous domains. Rather than a society unified by a common culture, Europe was a region torn apart by a mass of kings, counts, priests, and plunderers, all competing for power. However, in the century after the death of Charles the Bald, a new way of ordering society developed. Known as feudalism, it combined social, political, military, techno-logical, and religious aspects.

Europe under attack

In the late eighth and early ninth cen-turies CE, Christian Europe was under attack from raiders on three fronts. From the north, the Vikings came by warship along coasts and rivers; from the east, attacking at lightning speed and with great ferocity, rode parties of Magyar horsemen; and from the south, by sea and land from the territories bordering the Mediterranean, came Muslim raiders.

The Vikings often targeted churches and monasteries—not through anti-Christian zeal but because these places were the repositories of the greatest treasures. Between the 9th and 11th cen-turies CE, Viking raiders had a major effect on the development of mainland Europe, England, and Ireland (see box, page 816).

The Magyars (ancestors of modern Hungarians) probably came originally from the Ural Mountains of Russia and over the centuries traveled southward and westward. They reached the lowlands of the mid-Danube in the ninth century CE and first raided the eastern Frankish king-dom in 862 CE. Their most devastating raids took place between 895 and 955 CE, when raiding parties from the Hungarian plain penetrated deep into western Europe. The Magyars, superb horsemen and fearsome mounted archers, traveled hundreds of miles in search of plunder. They relied, like the Vikings, on the element of surprise; they attacked suddenly, seized booty, and then departed swiftly.

The ninth and tenth centuries CE were also the heyday of the Arab states bordering the Mediterranean. The period saw the establishment of the Fatimid caliphate in Africa, with its capital at Cairo. Muslim fleets controlled the seas; one Islamic writer claimed that the

Charles the Bald, depicted in this stained-glass window, ruled the western Frankish kingdom between 843 and 877 CE.

THE VIKINGS IN ENGLAND AND IRELAND

The first major Viking raid against England took place in 793 CE, when Norwegian marauders burned the monastery that had been established around 635 CE by Saint Aidan on the Island of Lindisfarne, off Northumberland, northeast England. Monks were slaughtered, and the treasures of the monastery were carried off. Two years later, Norwegian raiders attacked Ireland, where they set up colonies in Limerick, Waterford, and Wexford. The Vikings later established Dublin around 831 CE.

England, divided into many kingdoms, proved to be easy prey for Danish raiders between the 9th and the 11th centuries CE. At first, the Vikings only raided, making lightning attacks and carrying off booty. Later, however, they began to settle, establishing a large landholding in eastern and northeastern England; Alfred the Great (848–899 CE) was the first to put up significant resistance to the Viking invaders. Then, his son Edward the Elder (871–924 CE) won a series of victories, conquering Viking-held East Anglia and Viking-held parts of Mercia (roughly equivalent to the Midlands region of modern England).

After around 980 CE, the Danes fought back decisively under the leadership of their ruler, King Harold Bluetooth, and his son Sweyn. King Aethelred II of England was forced to pay a vast annual tribute in gold, called Danegeld. In the 11th century CE, a Danish king, Cnut (or Canute), ruled England and briefly established a Scandinavian empire containing England, Denmark, and Norway. After Cnut's death in 1035 CE, his dynasty was destroyed by infighting and the English throne passed to Edward the Confessor, Aethelred's son.

This gravestone at Lindisfarne depicts Viking raiders.

The tomb of the Viking raider Rollo lies at Notre Dame Cathedral in Rouen, France.

Christians could not "float a plank on the Mediterranean." Sailors invaded southern European countries seeking plunder and built permanent operating bases. In 827 CE, Arabs landed on the Mediterranean island of Sicily. Five years later, they captured its capital, Palermo, which they made into a glittering cosmopolitan city to rival Cairo. Arabs occupied part of southern Italy and around 889 CE established the base of Farakhshanit (Fraxinet) near modern St. Tropez in France.

A further threat to western Europe lay in the great ambitions of the Byzantine Empire. The Macedonian dynasty, whose first emperor was Basil I (ruled 867–886 CE), intervened in Italy, conquering territory in the south and establishing strongholds in Taranto and Bari.

Carolingian succession

The ostensible rulers of western Europe found the challenges difficult to overcome. In particular, those Carolingians who were the inheritors of Charlemagne's mantle in the western part of his empire generally proved to be unsuccessful rulers. Contemporaries emphasized

This 19th-century-CE illustration depicts Árpád, leader of the Magyars in the ninth century CE. During that period, the Magyars carried out many raids on central Europe.

the feebleness of many of their rulers by using vicious epithets. Louis the Stammerer, Charles the Bald's son and successor, died in 879 CE, a mere two years after this father. He left the throne of the western Frankish kingdom to his sons, Carloman and another Louis. Both died within five years, leaving their infant half brother, Charles the Simple, as the only heir to the throne.

Another Charles, known as Charles the Fat, had become the ruler of the eastern Frankish kingdom as the only remaining son of Louis the German. He took the crown from the baby Charles the Simple. In so doing, he reunited the Carolingian Empire, but only briefly. In the east, he was soon deposed by Arnulf, a grandson of Louis the German. In the west, power eventually fell back into the hands of Charles the Simple, who became king in 893 CE.

The Viking threat

Some victories were won over the Vikings, notably by Arnulf in 891 CE at the Dyle River near modern-day Brussels. However, other rulers were reduced to buying off Viking raiders. For example, in 911 CE, Charles the Simple gave territory in what became known as Normandy to the Viking leader Rollo, whose warriors had been harassing the area. In return, Rollo agreed to defend the area from raids by other bands of Vikings. The Carolingians had a rather ambivalent attitude to these raiders from the north. The Vikings were related to the Franks (both were part of the group of peoples who spoke Germanic languages), and the Vikings were happy to embrace the Christian faith when it suited them. For example, under the Treaty of Saint-Clair-sur-Epte, which established Viking territory in Normandy in 911 CE, Rollo was baptized as a Christian.

In the British Isles, Viking raiders either forcibly conquered areas or were given land. Although there were some periods when Anglo-Saxon monarchs were able to defeat the Viking forces (see box, page 816), most of what is now England was incorporated into the empire of the Viking ruler Sweyn Forkbeard in the early 11th century CE.

The lands that had formed the eastern part of Charlemagne's empire also suffered under raids from the Vikings and the Magyars. This area was divided into five large dukedoms: Saxony, Franconia, Swabia, Bavaria, and Lorraine. Having suffered severely during Viking raids in the ninth century CE, these dukedoms, particularly Saxony, bore the brunt of Magyar raids in the tenth century CE.

The rise of feudalism

During this period of political and military weakness, a brand new social structure emerged. It is known as feudalism, and it took different forms in the regions that became modern England, France, and Germany. However, there were common elements.

The feudal system developed from the patterns of land ownership and personal loyalty developed under Charles the Simple's Merovingian and Carolingian predecessors. Land in the form of fiefdoms was granted by lords to vassals, in return for military services and the fealty the vassals pledged to the lord. The land was worked by serfs (peasants who were tied to the land). Vassalage was an obligation owed to the lord in return for the right to a fiefdom. The lords, the great landowners, were themselves tied to the king as his vassals. As the wealth and power of the landowners increased, that of the king or emperor diminished. However, in the end,

Charles the Fat briefly united the eastern and western Frankish kingdoms in the ninth century CE. He is depicted here in a 19th-century-CE engraving.

ALFRED THE GREAT

Alfred, the youngest of the five sons of King Aethelwulf, succeeded his brother Aethelred as king of the West Saxons in 871 CE. The future looked grim; his kingdom and the whole of Anglo-Saxon England were at risk of being overrun by Danish invaders. However, Alfred succeeded in containing the Danish threat and establishing himself as the king of England. Like Charlemagne, he combined military prowess with an interest in learning and oversaw a great educational and cultural revival in his country. He is the only monarch in English history to be known as "the Great."

In 873 CE, Alfred made peace with the Danes. However, they invaded again in 877 CE and by early the following year had taken most of Wessex. Retreating into the countryside of Somerset, southwest England, Alfred waged guerrilla war while gathering his forces. In May of 878 CE, he won a resounding victory over the Danes in the Battle of Edington on Salisbury Plain.

The Danes pledged not to attack Wessex again and withdrew to an area of northeast England known as the Danelaw (roughly corresponding to East Anglia, the east Midlands, and Yorkshire). Alfred strengthened the defenses of his southern English kingdom of Wessex, building a series of fortified towns and reorganizing the army and navy. In 886 CE, he captured London and was recognized as king by all Englishmen not living in the Danelaw. He laid the foundations for a successful onslaught against the Danes by his son Edward.

Alfred promoted education; he established a court school and invited the leading scholars of the day to teach. They included the Welsh monk Asser and the Irish theologian John Scotus Erigena. Alfred decreed that all free-born children in England were to learn to read and write. He learned Latin and translated various documents into Anglo-Saxon, including Pope Gregory the Great's *Treatise on Pastoral Care* (which was given to English bishops to serve as a guide) and *The Consolation of Philosophy* by the Roman philosopher Boethius. Alfred also wrote the first new laws in more than a century; reflecting his interest in the integration of the country, these laws did not distinguish between the English and the Welsh.

Alfred also sponsored the creation of the *Anglo-Saxon Chronicle*, which unusually for the period was written in Anglo-Saxon rather than Latin and covered the history of England right back to the Roman invasion in the first century CE.

This statue of King Alfred the Great stands in the English city of Winchester. Winchester was the capital of Wessex.

everyone owed allegiance to someone. In the case of kings and emperors, it was owed to God himself.

The landowners became more powerful in the late ninth century CE. Charles the Bald, needing support in struggles against his brother Louis the German and against Viking raiders along coasts and rivers, declared many fiefs to be hereditary. The oath of allegiance to the king or emperor required in Charlemagne's time had within only two generations become a mere formality that was expected before a lord assumed his father's position.

During this period, as central authority failed, kings or emperors were forced to buy the support of nobles by giving away their own lands. In the end, they were left with little more than the palaces bequeathed to them by their royal fathers. Increasingly powerless, the kings could be made or broken by the region's great landowners.

The decline of freemen farmers

Faced with the collapse of imperial power and the threat of raiders on all sides, peasants and small landholders felt extremely vulnerable. Serfs on the great estates had the right to the protection, such as it was, that was guaranteed by landholders in the feudal relationship. Freemen, however, had no right to protection on the estates; they were mostly peasants who owned small pieces of farmland. Freemen, who had formed a considerable part of the population during the reign of Charlemagne, depended on the king for their protection. When Carolingian power disintegrated, the freemen were left exposed at a time of great unrest.

These freemen had to give up their freedom to get onto an estate and gain whatever protection was available there. A great mass of farmers who had once been independent lost their freedom and were

bought and sold, farms and all. By the 10th century CE, the class of free farmers had all but disappeared in some parts of Europe. Once on an estate, free farmers who brought their land with them became serfs, little different from the tenant farmers already on the estate.

The social pyramid in feudalism

The feudal universe was commonly viewed as a pyramid, with the peasants at the bottom, the clergy above the peasants,

This ninth-century-CE manuscript illustration depicts the various agricultural tasks that had to be performed in each of the 12 months of the year.

the nobility above the clergy, and God above them all. Within this scheme, each of the three main social groups had its task; according to one Dutch author from the Middle Ages, "the first bakes, the second prays, and the third wields the sword." Each person had his fixed position. It was a sin to seek to change one's social standing.

The feudal system was relatively static. Although the development of feudal society in Europe was a process that lasted hundreds of years (from the 10th century to the 13th century CE) and took on different aspects in various places, it was always marked by the defining of people in relation to the land and by an arrangement of social contracts that restricted people to the class and function by which they were categorized. Feudalism grew out of and then reinforced the economic and political conditions of Europe of the time.

Feudalism created a world in which everyone ostensibly had a social, political, and spiritual place. There were, however, certain fault lines that manifested themselves regularly during the medieval period. A key issue lay with the position of the church; disputes arose over whether the pope or the emperor had ultimate

control over appointing senior churchmen to positions. Another area of confusion concerned towns, where the simple relationship between a serf and his lord often did not exist. A further category of people who did not fit into the system were merchants.

Warfare and feudalism

In the sphere of warfare, feudalism was characterized by two major aspects that were closely linked: the use of heavy cavalrymen in battle and the emergence of castles. The lord was essentially a warrior fighting in armor, mounted on a heavy horse, and supported by vassals. His residence was a castle, to which his vassals could flee for safety when threatened.

The idea of the lord as a mounted warrior was central to the culture of feudalism. Particularly important was the idea of chivalry. The word *chivalry* itself comes from the French word *cheval*, meaning "horse." Chivalry involved a code of conduct that knights were expected to follow. The code involved obedience to one's lord, refusal to break an oath, and a willingness to fight to defend Christianity.

Feudal lords themselves had no centralized army to call on to keep raiders

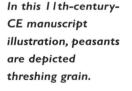

In this 11th-century-CE manuscript illustration, peasants are depicted threshing grain.

In this 14th-century-CE illustration, two knights approach Jerusalem during the First Crusade.

and plunderers at bay, so they developed the castle as part of their defenses. In its earliest form, the castle was far from the later impressive stone fortress, with its multiple towers and battlements. An early castle often consisted of little more than a drumlike residential tower of wood and loam with small openings for weaponry. The tower was often built on a motte, or artificial mound, surrounded by a circular defensive palisade and ditch. Castles did not only serve as a defense against barbarian raiders; they could also be used to defend an area against the armies of a centralized monarchy that might seek to diminish the authority of a local magnate.

Religion and feudalism

Feudalism was not just a social and military structure. The church's rulers, who had a stake in maintaining the status quo, made feudalism a part of Christian ideology. The network of mutual obligations in feudalism began as a response to economic forces. It then acquired political

LIFE IN A MEDIEVAL MANOR

The medieval manor was a self-supporting farming community. The lord who owned all the land subdivided it, retaining one section for himself and distributing the rest among the peasants who lived in the nearby village. The peasants' land was divided into strips, often some way apart from one another, so that both good and poor land was shared. In exchange for the right to cultivate their own sections, the peasants had to work the lord's land one or more days a week. In addition, they were often forced to pay the lord a fixed amount in kind, usually in grain, poultry, or eggs.

Most soil was quickly exhausted when it was used for uninterrupted cultivation of grain. Arable land was usually revitalized by leaving it fallow (unplanted) for some time and then grazing cattle on it. Often, the land was cultivated one year and then left fallow the next. This system was called two-course rotation. Sometimes, the peasants improved the land quality by covering the soil with peat cut from nearby bogs. Both of these procedures were eventually superseded by a system of three-course rotation; summer and winter crops were planted and harvested in succession, followed by a fallow period, after which the cycle was repeated.

Life was very hard for the serfs. They had a measure of protection and could take refuge within the manor house, or sometimes castle, but their farmland was liable to be damaged by armies or gangs of raiders—or even by local huntsmen or wild animals. Serfs could not be dismissed or driven off the land, although if they were caught poaching on the lord's lands, they might be maimed or put to death. On the other hand, they could not choose to move or marry without first seeking the lord's approval.

The serfs, who lived in cottages with earthen floors and thatched roofs, wore clothes of leather, wool, or linen. Their diet was basic; in northern Europe, serfs lived mainly on vegetables, oats, barley, and beer, while farther south, their counterparts had access to wheat and wine. Bound within the constraints of the feudal system, the peasants had little chance to change their position or improve their prospects.

SAINT BENEDICT AND THE MONASTIC IDEAL

The monk who would later be known as Saint Benedict was born into a noted Italian family around 480 CE. He rejected the licentiousness of life in Rome and retreated to a cave near Subiaco, 40 miles (64 km) east of the city. He lived there for three years, gaining a reputation as a holy man. He became abbot of a local monastery, but the monks disliked his stringent policies so much that one of them tried to poison him.

Subsequently, Benedict founded 12 local monasteries before establishing a celebrated monastic house at Monte Cassino (roughly midway between Naples and Rome). There, he set a standard of monastic life that was eventually adopted by most western monasteries. It called for monks to take vows of obedience, poverty, and chastity and established that they should divide the day into five or six hours of prayer, five hours of manual labor, and four hours of reading spiritual and biblical texts. Each monastery was governed by an abbot, whose role was like that of a father to the subordinate monks.

Saint Benedict gives a copy of his rules concerning monastic life to the monk Maurus. This illustration dates to the 12th century CE.

importance and became a social tradition. Finally, it came to be seen as a divinely sanctioned aspect of the world; the social contract of feudalism was presented as the will of God.

The church may have been seen as a separate social entity, distinct from the nobility and the peasantry, but in practice, its social composition was the same as that of the other groups. It drew its members from the general population, and its hierarchy reflected that of the larger society. The lower levels of the church hierarchy consisted of ordinary peasants, while the higher levels (the prelates and above) were of noble birth. It was customary for nobles to try to help relatives attain positions as bishops or abbots—often for relatively mundane reasons such as providing a means of support for their families. As a result, religious and secular lords frequently came from the same families and represented the same interests. Some requirements of the Christian priesthood, such as celibacy, were often ignored.

Because church appointments were made for political reasons, the men who were granted the highest spiritual offices were not always those most suited to the task. The effect was demoralizing, and

Jumièges Abbey in Normandy was built in the 11th century CE.

reform was badly needed. In many cases, the lifestyles that the monks and the abbots followed were far removed from the original ideal laid down by Saint Benedict (see box, page 824).

The abbey at Cluny

Some Christian laymen and priests were concerned about the state of the church. In 910 CE, the western Frankish count William of Aquitaine bestowed his hunting lands in Burgundy to a clergyman named Berno, so he could found a monastery. William hoped to create a model community that was not subject to the negative influences that were rife in many other existing monasteries.

William named the monastery Cluny, placing Abbot Berno and the abbey under the direct control of Pope Sergius III and his successors. Berno and his assistant (and eventual successor), Odo, created a model Christian world. The abbey's monks—and, from the 11th century CE, nuns—adhered to a stricter version of the Benedictine rule established in the sixth century CE by Saint Benedict.

The abbey at Cluny served as a model for monasteries across Europe.

Odo reformed monasteries throughout Europe so that they followed the model of Cluny, which offered support. These monasteries were granted the same independent status as the parent monastery except that they were directly accountable to Odo and his successors. Cluniac monks were renowned for their religious zeal. In contrast with the more regulated day of the Benedictines, who spent as much time in manual labor as they did at prayer, the Cluniacs spent almost all their time at prayer or in church services and therefore had laborers work the monastery lands on their behalf.

The Capetian dynasty

During the 10th century CE, the lands of the former western Frankish kingdom were divided among a number of powerful nobles, any one of whom could have defeated the king in battle. Such men as the lords of Burgundy, the counts of Anjou, and the dukes of Normandy (descendants of the Viking leader Rollo) made the crown no more than an ornament; the kings retained virtually no genuine power.

Charles the Simple reigned for almost 30 years before he was overthrown by his nobles in 922 CE. The crown passed through the hands of Robert I and Rudolf, duke of Burgundy, before falling to Charles's son, Louis from Overseas, in 936 CE. Louis got his nickname because he spent much of his childhood in England, for his own safety. He ruled as Louis IV until his death in 954 CE. Although Louis revived the standing of the ailing Carolingian dynasty, his son Lothair (ruled 954–986 CE) was unable to command the support of his powerful magnates. Lothair's son Louis V died after a reign of just two years (986–987 CE), and the combined forces of the nobility and the clergy gave the throne to Hugh Capet, count of Paris, who was a descendant of Duke Odo and King Robert I. Hugh's ally Adalbero, archbishop of Reims, had convinced the magnates to reject Charles of Lorraine, Louis V's uncle and the best-placed Carolingian successor to the crown.

Hugh's reign was marked by continued unrest among the magnates and repeated attempts by Charles of Lorraine to seize the throne. Nevertheless, Hugh survived, along with the Capetian dynasty. Shortly after becoming king, Hugh arranged to have his son Robert the Pious crowned king, appointing him as an associate to share the reign. The move set a precedent that was followed by all the Capetian kings until the end of the 12th century CE.

Robert succeeded his father in 996 CE without trouble and in turn named his own eldest son, Hugh Magnus, to succeed him. Robert II and Hugh Magnus ruled side by side from 1017 to 1025 CE. When Hugh died, his brother Henry became King Henry I. Henry ruled

Hugh Capet, depicted in this 13th-century-CE manuscript illustration, gave his name to the Capetian dynasty that ruled France.

DYNASTIC CHANGE

The Capetian dynasty followed the Carolingian dynasty, which ruled from 751 to 987 CE and ended with the reign of Louis V, whom Hugh Capet succeeded. The Carolingian dynasty is named after its celebrated kings named Charles, including Charles Martel and Charlemagne. The term *Carolingian* comes from the Latin form of Charles, *Carolus*.

Capetian kings ruled the western Frankish lands for more than 300 years, from 987 and 1328 CE. The dynasty took its name from Hugh Capet's surname, which was derived from the Latin word *capa*, meaning "cape." However, the dynasty's founder is sometimes identified as either Hugh's grandfather Robert I, who ruled very briefly from 922 to 923 CE, or Hugh's great-uncle, Odo, who ruled from 888 to 898 CE. Both Odo and Robert spent much of their reigns in conflict with Carolingian kings. Others identify the founder of the Capetian dynasty as Duke Robert the Strong, the father of both Odo and Robert.

After Hugh Capet, the Capetians continued to hand down the crown through a direct male line until 1328 CE, when Charles IV died with no male heirs. A related family, the Valois, took over France for the next 250 years.

alongside his father until Robert died in 1031 CE. Afterward, Henry reigned alone until 1059 CE and beside his own son Philip I between 1059 and 1060 CE. Many historians identify the start of the Capetian dynasty as the point at which the western Frankish territory, formerly known as Francia Occidentalis, can finally be seen as modern France—partially because Hugh was originally the count of Paris and made the city his capital.

The Capetian kings gained land through marriage and wanted to hold on to it. If landholdings were to remain intact, guaranteed to be passed down undivided through the family, the right to inheritance had to be honored. Then, to ensure that the land was not divided, the principles of primogeniture (inheritance by the first son rather than by all sons equally) and the indivisibility of land had to be accepted. The first of these concepts, the right to inheritance, had been invoked by vassals of the feudal system since the ninth century CE in order to

On the left in this 14th-century-CE manuscript illustration, Henry I of France asks Robert of Normandy for help. On the right, Henry besieges a town.

retain familial control of fiefdoms. The Capetians used this practice to justify the retention of their crown and their lands. The other two ideas were breaches in the system of feudalism. The Capetians undermined that system and rose to dominance by acquiring control of most of the western Frankish territories by assimilating additional fiefdoms into their lands and then applying the principles of primogeniture and the indivisibility of land.

The eastern Frankish region

As in the western Frankish lands, power in the separate dukedoms of the eastern Frankish lands became concentrated in the hands of one duke, Conrad of Franconia, who was elected king of the eastern Frankish territories in 911 CE. Conrad replaced Louis the Child, who was the last Carolingian ruler in the east.

Conrad ruled as King Conrad I until 918 CE, spending most of the reign fighting Slav and Magyar raiders and combat-

ing his own dukes; in his time, the Magyars plundered as far as Burgundy and Lotharingia. Conrad's successor, chosen by Frankish and Saxon nobles, was Duke Henry of Saxony, who became known as Henry the Fowler because he reputedly heard of his elevation to the kingship while out hunting.

Henry the Fowler, ruling as King Henry I, greatly strengthened the eastern Frankish realm. While allowing the dukes of Swabia and Bavaria to continue to rule their domains, he forced them to accept his authority. After a military campaign in 925 CE, he brought Lotharingia (independent since 910 CE) back within the

This 19th-century-CE illustration depicts Henry the Fowler, who became Henry I.

eastern Frankish realm. In 926 CE, he agreed to pay tribute to the Magyars in return for a nine-year truce; he used the time to build up the defenses of Saxon villages and to train troops of mounted warriors. Many of the fortified towns later developed into cities, including Merseburg, Nordhausen, and Goslar. In 933 CE, Henry used his cavalry to defeat the Magyars at the Battle of Riade near the Unstrut River.

By the time Henry died in 936 CE, he had become the most powerful man in the territories of the former Carolingian Empire and had created a united kingdom in the eastern Frankish realm. Historians usually identify the reigns of Henry I and his son Otto I as the beginning of modern Germany.

Otto the Great

Henry's son and successor, Otto, set out to impose his authority on rebellious vassals, defeating Frankish, Bavarian, and Lotharingian nobles and replacing them with his own followers and relatives. He also planned to establish his authority over the higher clergy and to use the church to stabilize his regime. He granted bishops and abbots extensive lands in the form of fiefdoms and newly created bishoprics.

The key to Otto's scheme was that the clergy were not allowed to marry; at this time, bishops and abbots—though officially celibate—did have children. However, because they could not marry, the children were by definition illegitimate, with no right of succession. Clerics, therefore, could never create a dynasty to rival the royal throne; the land granted in fief would always be returned to the king. The bishoprics Otto created, and the lands he granted in fief were centers of royal authority; he used ambitious prelates to undermine the authority

The nobleman Berengar II of Ivrea begs the Frankish king Otto I for help in this illustration that was created around 1150 CE.

of the secular lords and to strengthen his own position.

Otto's reign perfectly reflected the various aspects of feudalism. Apart from his incorporation of the church into the structure of his state, he also used heavy cavalry to great effect on the battlefield. At the Battle of Lechfeld, near Augsburg in 955 CE, Otto won a decisive victory over the Magyars during a bloody three-day encounter. The lightly armored Magyar horse archers found that their arrows were ineffective against Otto's armored knights, and the Magyars were ridden down when they came into hand-to-hand combat. The battle ended the Magyar threat; the horsemen never troubled Germany again.

In the following years, Otto continued to establish his authority through military means. In a series of campaigns against the Slavs between 955 and 960 CE, he broke their independence in the regions of the Oder and Elbe rivers. In Italy, he established himself as king of the Lombards after invading in 951 CE and was crowned emperor in Rome in 962 CE. After his coronation, only kings from the eastern Frankish region were crowned emperor. They based their claims to rule not only Italy but all Christians on the achievements of the ruler remembered as Otto the Great.

See also:

The Carolingian Empire (volume 6, page 804) •
The Holy Roman Empire (volume 6, page 832)

In this 19th-century-CE woodcut, Otto I is depicted leading his troops at the Battle of Lechfeld.

THE HOLY ROMAN EMPIRE

During the 10th and 11th centuries CE, the rulers of the emerging country of Germany came into conflict with the pope over whether the state or the church had the right to make religious appointments.

The late 9th and early 10th centuries CE had seen the collapse of Charlemagne's empire and devastating raids on western Europe by Vikings from the north, by Saracens from the south, and by Magyars from the east. In the middle of the 10th century CE, however, two rulers of the eastern section of the former Frankish empire—Henry I (ruled 919–936 CE) and Otto I (ruled 936–973 CE)—succeeded in creating a strong and unified kingdom. Henry and Otto expanded their control southward into Italy to form a new empire. The unified country over which they presided is now regarded as the beginning of modern Germany, and their empire is called the German Empire. This empire was smaller than Charlemagne's had been; it did not include the western Frankish lands (from around this time identified by historians as France). The new empire amounted to Germany and northern Italy, with the later addition of Burgundy.

Emperor of Rome

Otto II ruled as joint emperor with his father from 967 CE and then, after Otto I's death, reigned alone until 983 CE. In 972 CE, Otto II married Theophanu, niece of the Byzantine emperor John I Tzimisces. Otto had to suppress a rebellion initiated by his cousin Henry II, duke of Bavaria, and to defend Lorraine against invasion by Lothair, king of France. Otto put down the Bavarian revolt in 978 CE. He then laid siege to Paris; he failed to capture the city, but the damage his army caused on its advance through northern France deterred Lothair from further invasions. In 980 CE, Lothair signed a treaty by which he formally abandoned his claim to Lorraine.

In spite of his marriage to a Byzantine princess, Otto II was in increasingly open conflict with the Byzantine (or eastern Roman) Empire. To strengthen his position at the head of the western empire, Otto declared himself "Roman emperor"—the first of Charlemagne's successors to use this title. In 980 CE, Otto led an army into southern Italy to counter Byzantine expansion and inroads made by Arab raiders. Otto captured Naples, Salerno, and Taranto but was defeated by a Muslim army at the Battle of Cotrone in 982 CE. The following year, shortly before his own death in Rome, Otto had his three-year-old son crowned as king of the Germans.

Emperor of the world

Otto III was too young to govern, so his Byzantine mother served as regent from 984 CE until her death in 991 CE. The

The German imperial orb and ceremonial sword date from the 12th century CE.

THE HOLY ROMAN EMPIRE

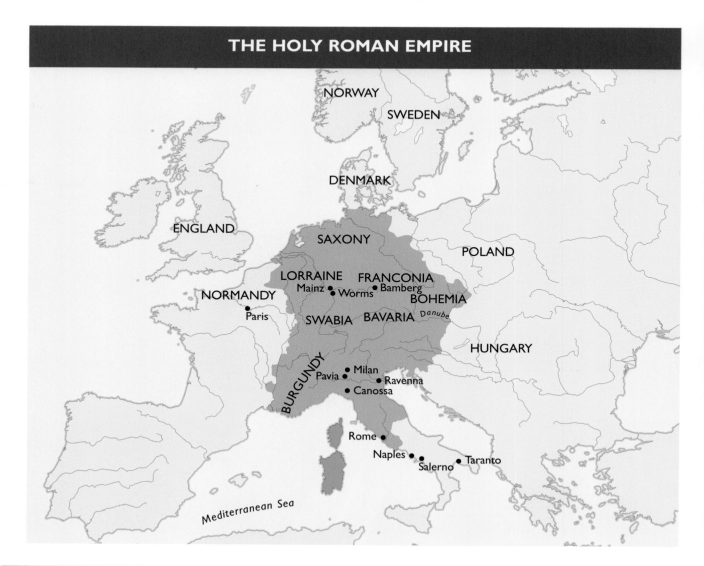

KEY

Extent of the Holy Roman Empire in 1175 CE

king was still only 11 years old, so his grandmother, Queen Adelaide, took over as regent in concert with Willigis, archbishop of Mainz; they stood down in 994 CE, when Otto reached his majority at age 14. Two years later, Otto III marched into Italy in response to an appeal from Pope John XV (ruled 985–996 CE), who needed help to put down a revolt. On the way to Rome, Otto was crowned king of the Lombards at Pavia, but by the time he reached Rome, the pope had died. Otto then had his cousin, Bruno of Carinthia, elected as Pope Gregory V (ruled 996–999 CE) and was himself crowned emperor. Otto's ambition was to unite the papacy, the

Roman Empire, and the Byzantine Empire in a universal Christian empire governed from Rome, with the emperor ruling supreme and having authority even over the pope.

Otto established his court in Rome, revived several ancient Roman customs, and insisted on Byzantine-style court ceremonies. He declared himself "Emperor of the world" and "Servant of Jesus Christ," thereby promoting himself as supreme ruler in both secular and spiritual realms. On the death of Gregory V, Otto demonstrated the emperor's ascendancy over the papacy by having his former tutor, Gerbert of Aurillac, elected as Pope Sylvester II.

In 1001 CE, Otto put down a revolt in the town of Tibur (present-day Tivoli) in Italy but spared the inhabitants. This act of mercy provoked a revolt in Rome, whose citizens wanted their rival townspeople to be punished as severely as they thought they would have been themselves in comparable circumstances. Unable to regain control of Rome, Otto retreated to a monastery at Ravenna to do penance. He then called for help from his cousin Henry, duke of Bavaria. Before Henry's troops arrived, Otto died in January of 1002 CE at the age of only 22. Contemporary sources suggested that he had contracted malaria in the marshes around Ravenna.

Church reformer and saint

Henry of Bavaria was elected King Henry II of Germany in July of 1002 CE, despite the opposition of many nobles and with the help of Otto's former ally Archbishop Willigis of Mainz. In 1004 CE, Henry invaded northern Italy, defeating Arduin of Ivrea, the self-styled king of Italy, and receiving the crown and title himself at Pavia. In the east, Henry waged a 14-year battle against King Boleslav I of Poland, and in the peace settlement of 1018 CE, Henry regained the German territory of Bohemia. Before that, in February of 1014 CE, Henry had been crowned emperor by Pope Benedict VII (ruled 1012–1024 CE). Henry's coronation was the first at which the new emperor held the imperial orb (a sphere made of jewels and precious metals and topped with a cross).

A lifelong supporter of church reform, Henry developed the system of the religious state pioneered by Otto I. Like Otto, Henry made substantial land grants to bishoprics and appointed loyal followers as bishops, using the church hierarchy to increase his own power over the secular nobility. Henry's most enduring achievement was the foundation of a

bishopric at Bamberg, a small town in Bavaria near the upper part of the Main River. Bamberg quickly grew into an important cathedral city and a center of learning.

In 1022 CE, at the Pope's request, Henry launched another campaign in Italy, defeating the Byzantine Greeks and the Lombards before returning north. With Pope Benedict VII, Henry planned a synod at Pavia to confirm elements of

This relief carving from the 11th century CE shows Otto II blessing his subjects. The function was traditionally performed only by the clergy.

A NEW ROMAN EMPIRE

The term "Holy Roman Empire" is used to describe the European territories that were united under Charlemagne and governed in various forms by Frankish and German rulers until 1806 CE. However, any use of the term to describe the period before the 13th century CE is no more than a convention; the name did not exist until 1254 CE, when the Latin form, *Sacrum Romanum Imperium*, came into usage. Moreover, the title was never official.

Charlemagne was crowned by Pope Leo III on Christmas day in 800 CE in a conscious revival of the western Roman Empire; both he and his father, Pépin, also held the title "Protector of the Romans." Otto II adopted the title "Roman Emperor," and the name "Roman Empire" was used for territories held by Conrad II in 1034 CE. The term "Holy Empire" was first used in 1157 CE. From 1512 CE, the empire was called the Holy Roman Empire of the German Nation.

This illustration from the late 10th century CE depicts Otto III at his coronation.

First king of the Salian dynasty

In Germany, Conrad of Franconia, a descendant of Otto the Great, was elected to succeed Henry II. He was crowned King Conrad II in 1024 CE in Mainz, then king of Italy in 1026 CE in Milan. Having put down revolts in northern Italy and Rome, Conrad was crowned emperor at Easter in 1027 CE by Pope John XIX (ruled 1024–1032 CE). Under an earlier agreement with Henry II, Conrad inherited the kingdom of Burgundy from Rudolf III (ruled 993–1032 CE). The inheritance significantly enlarged the emperor's landholdings and prestige. It also established a link between the empire's German and Italian territories, which had previously been separated by Burgundy.

The expansion of imperial power in Italy and Burgundy was matched by its gains in the east during the late 10th century and the 11th century CE. As early as the reign of Henry I, Saxon settlers had been encouraged to move east and organize themselves in well-defended towns. The settlers conducted a series of campaigns against the Slavs and the Magyars. Conrad continued this expansion, winning territory from the Poles and, in 1035 CE, defeating the pagan Liutitians. Not all of Conrad's campaigns

their church reforms. However, Henry died in 1024 CE before this convention could take place. In recognition of his good works, Henry was canonized in 1146 CE, 22 years after his death; he is the only German king to have been made a saint.

ended in triumph, however; in 1029 CE, he was defeated by, and had to cede land to, King Stephen I of Hungary.

Conrad had to contend with revolts among the nobility, and he adopted an unusual means of dealing with them. He supported the lower nobility against the powerful dukes and, by doing so, secured direct rule over most of the duchies; only Saxony and Lorraine remained independent. Conrad's position became so strong that he was able to secure the succession of his son, Henry, without an election. The pattern of a hereditary crown in the House of Conrad (also known as the Salian dynasty) continued for a century.

The emperor dominates the pope

From the start of his reign in 1039 CE, Henry III demonstrated his support for the church reform movement (see box, page 838). At first, he was busy defending his Polish vassals against invading Bohemians and restoring to power the deposed king of Hungary, but in 1046 CE, Henry traveled to Rome to be crowned emperor. His coronation ended a conflict between three rival contenders for the papacy. Benedict IX had abdicated and sold his office to a wealthy supporter of church reform who attempted to reign as Pope Gregory VI. Benedict then tried to revive his rule, while a third churchman, Bishop John of Sabina, won election to the papacy and attempted to reign as Pope Sylvester III. Henry III deposed all three rivals and appointed the German bishop of Bamberg as Pope Clement II.

The papacy was now under the control of the emperor. Over the course of his reign, Henry III appointed three more popes, all of whom were German. Henry's donation of large areas of land to monasteries and prelates and his commitment to church reform made the role of emperor more highly regarded than

that of the pope in the eyes of leading church reformers, such as the abbots of Cluny. Images from the period show the emperor, rather than the pope, as the spiritual heir of the apostle Saint Peter and as God's lieutenant on earth.

In the last 10 years of his reign, Henry III failed to maintain control over his empire and lost great swathes of territory in southern Italy, Lorraine, Hungary, and northeastern Germany. His church reforms began to unravel, partly because he had too few clerical allies in Germany. Some accounts suggest that, toward the end of his life, Henry was no longer fully fit to govern, perhaps in the aftermath of a severe illness that struck him in 1045

This 11th-century-CE manuscript illumination depicts two bishops standing on either side of Henry II of Germany.

CHURCH REFORM

During the 250 years that followed the foundation of the abbey at Cluny in 910 CE, the Cluniac order exerted a major influence on western European religious life and thought. New monasteries were set up along Cluniac lines, and many existing foundations followed Cluny's practices. Because all Cluniac monasteries were answerable to the abbot of Cluny, he became one of the most important men in Christendom, second only to the pope. At the height of Cluny's power, in the mid-12th century CE, its abbot controlled more than 1,500 priories and monasteries. The Cluniac Reform Movement aimed to eliminate simony (the sale of church offices), reimpose celibacy on the priesthood, and end secular appointments to church positions. The reforms were supported by several popes, including Leo IX and Gregory VII.

The Roman church, which had previously encouraged stability, began to promote the need for change. There was a genuine drive in monasteries to emulate the Cluniac model, and elsewhere, clergymen who had been granted their positions by secular authorities came under increasing pressure; the church even supported uprisings against bishops of the old order. In the new climate, ordinary laymen were encouraged to express their opinions. Soon, members of the laity began to put forward criticisms of the church hierarchy that went farther than even the most radical reformers wanted. Some of the new ideas focused not on the political and institutional problems of the church but on the correct interpretation of the *vita apostolica* (the apostolic life)— the correct way to live as Christ's apostles did.

The abbey at Cluny is still an active monastery. It is situated near Mâcon, the most southerly town in Burgundy.

CE. Henry III died in Germany in 1056 CE. He was succeeded by his six-year-old son, Henry IV, who had been elected king in 1054 CE.

The Great Schism

The election of Henry IV coincided with one of the most momentous events in the history of Christianity—the final break between the church based in Constantinople and the church based in Rome. The Great Schism (see box, page 840) took place at a time when both Rome and Constantinople were sending missions into eastern and northern Europe, converting pagan peoples to Christianity. The conversion process was often a result of political conquest, and in the case of areas such as Bohemia and Poland, the influence of the Roman church predominated because of the power of the German emperors. In other parts of Europe, such as Bulgaria and Russia, Greek Orthodox Christianity was adopted. Although there was resistance to Christianization of pagan areas, many local rulers saw that they could turn Christianity to personal advantage by using it to extend their own authority; it was one thing to govern by hereditary right and force of arms but another, greater, thing to rule by the grace of God.

Investiture controversy

Some leading churchmen—notably supporters of the deposed Gregory VI—dreamed of a church that was free from interference by the laity. One of the most influential of these churchmen was Gregory's chaplain, Hildebrand of Soana (a small town in present-day Tuscany, Italy). The group saw the accession of the child-emperor Henry IV as an opportunity to fight back against the emperor's power to appoint the pope. At a church

council in Rome in 1059 CE, they agreed a scheme for electing the pope by a college of clergymen (later cardinals). Their objective was to deny the emperor and lay nobility any role in the appointment of the head of the Roman church.

In 1073 CE, Hildebrand became Pope Gregory VII. He was put on the papal throne by the popular acclamation of the people of Rome while the college of cardinals was preparing to elect a new pope. His efforts both before and after his elevation to the papacy comprise what is called the Gregorian Reform; he asserted the primacy of the papacy over secular authority. Members of this reform movement were keen to eliminate simony (the sale of church offices) because it was used by the emperor and other lay figures to install their own followers in key positions in the church.

Gregory VII took full advantage of the weakness of the young Henry IV,

The official seal of Conrad II carries a likeness of the king.

THE GREAT SCHISM

In 1054 CE, the leaders of the western and eastern Christian churches, Pope Leo IX in Rome and Patriarch Michael Cerularius in Constantinople, excommunicated each other. The split between the two branches of the church, which endured despite later attempts at reconciliation, is known as the Great Schism.

The origins of the quarrel can be traced back to at least the fifth century CE; there had been tension between Constantinople and Rome since the fall of Rome in 476 CE, when the pope (or the bishop of Rome, by his Byzantine title) was left as the protector of western Christianity. Rome was the burial place of the apostle Peter (who, according to the Bible, was the "rock" on which

Christ intended to establish his church), and Roman popes claimed direct succession to Peter and "apostolic" primacy over any ecumenical council. The eastern patriarchs respected that tradition but claimed supremacy because Constantinople was the seat of both the Byzantine emperor and the church senate; those were described as the actual or "pragmatic" factors. These different views of primacy—apostolic versus pragmatic—were debated again in the 11th century CE.

Another source of disagreement concerned the question of whether the Holy Spirit came from God the Father alone or from God the Father and God the Son (Jesus Christ). The western church incorporated the word *filioque* (and from the Son) into the Nicene Creed, or statement of faith, so that one part of it read: "I believe in the Holy Spirit, who proceeds from the Father and the Son." The *filioque* clause was introduced in Spain in the seventh century CE and accepted and promoted by Charlemagne from 800 CE. Although the clause was opposed for many years by the papacy, it was accepted in 1014 CE, but in the eastern church, it was considered a heresy. Other differences concerned clerical celibacy (the eastern church allowed married men to be ordained as priests, but the western church insisted on lifelong abstinence from sex) and the use of unleavened bread in Holy Communion (the western church allowed it, but the eastern church did not). Those disputes could not be settled because of the overriding disagreement about the ultimate source of judgment. The papacy claimed to be infallible, the final authority, while the eastern church invoked a conciliar principle, based on the authority of councils, in which even local churches had a voice.

The present Bamberg Cathedral was built in Romanesque style. The original, founded by Henry II in 1004 CE, was destroyed by fire 77 years later.

whose reign began with an ineffective regency (1056–1065 CE) by his mother, Agnes, and who was then forced to quell a rebellion in Saxony. Gregory put through strong reforms at the Roman Synod of 1075 CE to eliminate simony, promote clerical celibacy, and forbid the appointment of church officials (investiture) by secular rulers. He regarded investiture (a term that referred to the presentation of symbols of office to church officials, as well as the appointment) as an exclusive church right. The synod formalized the outbreak of the "investiture controversy," which was effectively a struggle between pope and emperor for control of the church.

Gregory VII and Henry IV had first disagreed over clerical appointments in Milan in 1073 CE. When the Patarines, a group of Milanese tradesmen, defied papal authority by electing an archbishop, Henry had his own appointee consecrated by Lombard bishops. Gregory then excommunicated the bishops, while Henry—still stretched by the Saxon rebellion—backed down and asked the pope to settle the problem. However, after Henry defeated the Saxons in 1075 CE, he put forward his court chaplain for the archbishopric, knowing that, in doing so, he risked open conflict with the papacy.

Gregory responded with a stern letter but offered to negotiate; Henry instead convened a council of German bishops at Worms (in southwestern Germany), where it was ordered that Gregory should be deposed. Henry sent the pope a letter addressed to "the false monk Hildebrand." The pope retaliated by excommunicating Henry, which meant that the emperor was excluded from the

This 19th-century-CE woodcut shows Henry III installing Pope Clement II.

This 19th-century-CE woodcut depicts Pope Gregory VII.

community of believers and that his subjects were not obliged to keep oaths they had made to him. The excommunication released Henry's subjects from their allegiance to him and seriously undermined his authority. The only way back was through papal forgiveness.

The road to Canossa

A coalition of German nobles met at Tribur in October of 1076 CE and threatened to rebel against Henry unless the king secured absolution within 12 months. There were even plans for a diet (formal assembly) at Augsburg to which

Gregory himself would be invited. Henry realized that he had no choice but to humble himself before the pope. He traveled to the castle of Canossa, in northern Italy, where Gregory was staying. Clad in a rough hair shirt and standing barefoot in the snow, the king prayed and fasted in the cold outside the castle gate. Only after three days of this penance did Gregory let him in—probably reluctantly, because the pope now had no choice but to offer forgiveness; by his own theological convictions, he was bound to forgive a repentant sinner. In the short term, the pope's forgiveness averted disaster for Henry, but it also changed permanently the dynamic of the relationship between the emperor and the papacy.

Civil war

The investiture conflict was not yet over. Feeling betrayed by the pope and being convinced that Henry was playing a trick, the German nobles issued a false version of the absolution at Canossa and elected Rudolf, duke of Swabia, as king in Henry's place. Their actions led to civil war in Germany. In March of 1080 CE, Gregory VII recognized the claims of Rudolf, excommunicated Henry again, and commanded that the king should be deposed. This time, royal repentance would not work; there was to be no second Canossa.

After Henry won the civil war, he settled his score with Gregory. Henry declared Gregory deposed and nominated Guibert, archbishop of Ravenna, as Pope Clement III. Rudolf of Swabia was killed in battle against Henry's forces in October of 1080 CE. Between 1081 and 1084 CE, Henry attacked Rome three times, on the third occasion capturing the city and having Guibert enthroned as Pope Clement III. The new pope crowned Henry emperor on March 31, 1084 CE. Pope Gregory fled to Salerno, where he died in May of 1085 CE.

Henry returned to Germany where, in 1098 CE, he had his 12-year-old son Henry elected as King Henry V. Six years later, when the German nobility threatened to revolt again, Henry V sided with the rebels, claiming that he owed no allegiance to an excommunicated parent. He imprisoned his father and, in December of 1105 CE, forced him to abdicate. Henry IV escaped and defeated his son's army in early 1106 CE. However, he died soon afterward, and the throne of Germany passed to Henry V.

The struggle continues

In 1106 CE, Henry V had to address the investiture question again after Pope Paschal II (ruled 1099–1118 CE) issued a decree renewing the prohibition on investiture. The two sides subsequently agreed that the emperor would honor the

This oil painting by Eduard Schwoiser (1826–1902 CE) shows Henry IV during his penance at Canossa.

decree if the pope would crown him and turn over the papacy's secular holdings to the Holy Roman Empire. When the terms of this bargain emerged, the people of Rome rose in rebellion. Henry, already in Rome for the coronation, took Paschal prisoner. After holding the pope in captivity for 61 days, the emperor got his way. Paschal agreed to crown Henry and guaranteed the emperor the right to conduct investitures. Henry V was duly installed as Holy Roman emperor in the Basilica of Saint Peter, Rome, in April of 1111 CE.

After the coronation, Henry, convinced that the investiture conflict was satisfactorily resolved, withdrew to Germany. However, he had misjudged the situation. In October of 1111 CE, he was excommunicated by papal legates in Germany; in March of 1112 CE, a coun-

cil declared the pope's previous concessions on investiture to be void because they had been made under duress. Henry returned to Rome, drove out Paschal, and had himself crowned again by Maurice Bourdin, archbishop of Braga. When Paschal died in 1118 CE, Pope Gelasius II was elected to succeed him. Henry instead declared Maurice Bourdin pope, as Gregory VIII. Henry was excommunicated once more, this time by Gelasius II.

Most of the German nobles were in open revolt against Henry, but the emperor made peace with them at the Diet of Würzburg in 1121 CE. A year later, Henry signed the Concordat (or treaty) of Worms with Pope Calixtus II (ruled 1119–1124 CE) to bring a temporary peace in the dispute over investiture. The agreement, which had been negotiated by the German nobles,

Henry IV's decisive victory over Rudolf of Swabia in 1080 CE is captured in this drawing by German artist Wilhem Camphausen (1818–1885 CE).

set out precise rules for investiture procedures. In Italy and Burgundy, bishops and abbots were to receive their spiritual regalia from a superior of the church. Only after that had happened would they receive their secular regalia from a representative of the emperor. In Germany, the order of events was to be reversed; abbots and bishops would receive their secular regalia first, followed by the ecclesiastical symbols. Henry was no longer able to make his own appointments to bishoprics; instead, chapters (ecclesiastical colleges) were established to elect new bishops. Henry would have the deciding vote if an election failed to produce a result. Henry abandoned Gregory VIII, and his excommunication was lifted.

Henry V died childless in Utrecht in 1125 CE. The last of the Salian dynasty of emperors, he was succeeded by one of the nobles who had previously rebelled against him, Duke Lothair III of Saxony.

Historical significance

Henry IV's journey to Canossa and his humiliation in the snow outside Pope Gregory's castle appeared to be a tremendous defeat, the lowest point in the history of the Salian dynasty. Some 800 years later, German Chancellor Otto von Bismarck said, "We will not go to Canossa," meaning that he was not prepared to yield to his opponents. Yet the famous incident is open to more than one interpretation. It is possible that Henry IV's actions were a clever ruse to put Gregory VII in a moral dilemma. The emperor may well have realized that the pope could never refuse absolution to a repentant sinner. Henry had only to show contrition, nothing else—not even goodwill. Perhaps Henry's repentance was no more than a political maneuver. While that seems possible, most modern historians agree that, in the longer term, Canossa severely weakened the standing of the emperor. By doing penance to

Gregory, Henry admitted that the papacy's position on church appointments was legal, which led to the loss of the empire's hard-won supremacy over the Holy See.

This gold relief of Henry V was placed on the tomb of Charlemagne in Aachen, Germany, after Henry's death.

See also:

The Carolingian Empire (volume 6, page 804)
• Feudal Europe (volume 6, page 814)

TIME LINE

WESTERN ASIA, NORTHERN AFRICA, AND EUROPE		REST OF THE WORLD	
208 CE	Ardashir I crowned king of Persis.	220 CE	Second Han period ends in China.
224 CE	Ardashir defeats Parthian king Artabanus at Battle of Hormuz.		
c. 240 CE	Prophet Mani has vision urging him to spread new religious faith.		
241 CE	Ardashir dies; Shapur I succeeds him.		
251 CE	Goths cross Danube and defeat Decius.		
260 CE	Shapur defeats Roman emperor Valerian at Edessa; Valerian spends rest of life in captivity.		
c. 320 CE		c. 320 CE	Gupta dynasty begins in India.
325 CE	Shapur II comes to power after 16-year regency.		
511 CE	Clovis I, founder of Merovingian dynasty, dies.		
531 CE	Khosrow I becomes king of Persia.	c. 550 CE	Buddhism imported to Japan from Korea. Kiev emerges as leading city in Russia.
570 CE	Prophet Mohammed born.		
610 CE	Mohammed begins to experience visions; in one vision, he is told that he is the Messenger of God.		

WESTERN ASIA, NORTHERN AFRICA, AND EUROPE		REST OF THE WORLD	
613 CE	Mohammed begins to preach publicly in Mecca.		
622 CE	Mohammed flees Mecca on September 20 with 100 followers; date of flight (or hegira) subsequently celebrated by Muslims.	**618 CE**	Chinese Tang period begins after overthrow of Sui dynasty.
624 CE	Mohammed defeats Meccans at Battle of Badr.		
629 CE	Mohammed leads first pilgrimage to Mecca.		
632 CE	Mohammed dies; Abu Bakr succeeds him as spiritual head of Islam.		
636 CE	Bedouin warriors defeat Byzantine forces at Battle of Yarmuk River.		
c. 650 CE		**c. 650 CE**	Paper money first circulated in China around this time.
651 CE	Death of Yazdegerd III marks end of Sassanid Empire.		
656 CE	Assassination of caliph Othman ibn Affan sparks rivalry for succession between Umayyads and descendants of the prophet Mohammed.		
661 CE	Umayyads establish first caliphate with Damascus as capital.	**c. 675 CE**	Srivijaya kingdom starts to dominate maritime trade around Malay Archipelago.
680 CE	Battle of Karbala causes lasting rift between Shi'ite and Sunni Muslims.		

WESTERN ASIA, NORTHERN AFRICA, AND EUROPE		REST OF THE WORLD	
687 CE	Frankish ruler Pépin gains victory at Battle of Testry.		
		702 CE	Japan adopts state system similar to that of China as result of Taika Reforms.
710 CE	Arabs capture Samarkand.	**710 CE**	Heijo becomes Japan's first fixed capital.
711 CE	Arabs cross from northern Africa; begin conquest of Spain.		
717 CE	Byzantine emperor Leo III repels Arab attack on Constantinople.		
732 CE	Arab advance into Europe halted by Charles Martel at Battle of Tours.		
c. 750 CE **750 CE**	Abu al-Abbas defeats Umayyads at Battle of Great Zab River; start of Abbasid dynasty.	**c. 750 CE**	Pala dynasty begins in Bengal. Teotihuacán destroyed by fire in Mexico.
762 CE	Al-Mansur transfers capital of caliphate to Baghdad from Damascus.		
768 CE	Charlemagne becomes co-ruler of Franks.		
771 CE	Charlemagne becomes sole king of Franks on death of brother Carloman.		
775 CE	Al-Mahdi becomes caliph; Baghdad begins growing toward height of power, wealth, and influence.		
782 CE	Monk Alcuin begins to teach at Aachen.		

	WESTERN ASIA, NORTHERN AFRICA, AND EUROPE		REST OF THE WORLD
	786 CE	Harun al-Rashid becomes caliph; reigns until 809 CE.	
	793 CE	Vikings destroy monastery on island of Lindisfarne off coast of England.	
	794 CE	Charlemagne makes Aachen capital of empire.	
c. 800 CE	**800 CE**	Charlemagne crowned Holy Roman emperor by Pope Leo III.	**c. 800 CE** Khmer state begins to flourish in present-day Cambodia. Maya from Guatemalan lowlands move to highlands and into Yucatán Peninsula. Chimú kingdom becomes powerful on coast of Peru. Polynesians settle in New Zealand.
	804 CE	Charlemagne finally subdues Saxons.	
	813 CE	Al-Mamun becomes caliph; encourages study of Greek philosophy. Charlemagne crowns only surviving son, Louis, co-emperor.	
	814 CE	Charlemagne dies; son Louis the Pious inherits empire.	
	817 CE	Louis issues *Ordinatio imperii*, dividing empire among his three sons.	
	830 CE	Three eldest sons rebel against Louis.	
	832 CE	Al-Mamun founds Bayt al-Hikma (House of Wisdom) in Baghdad.	
	c. 833 CE	Einhard completes *Life of Charlemagne*.	
	886 CE	Alfred the Great becomes king of England.	

WESTERN ASIA, NORTHERN AFRICA, AND EUROPE		REST OF THE WORLD	
893 CE	Charles the Simple inherits crown of western Frankish kingdom.	**c. 900 CE**	Toltecs become major power in central and southern Mexico. Start of Postclassic period.
910 CE	Monastery founded at Cluny.		
911 CE	Charles gives area of north-western France to Viking leader Rollo; it becomes Duchy of Normandy.		
945 CE	Shi'ite Buyids seize power in Baghdad.		
955 CE	Otto I defeats Magyars at Battle of Lechfeld.		
962 CE	Otto I crowned Roman emperor.		
980 CE	Avicenna born in Bukhara.		
987 CE	Hugh Capet, count of Paris, becomes king of western Frankish lands.		
996 CE	Otto III installs Pope Gregory V.		
c. 1000 CE		**c. 1000 CE**	Leif Eriksson lands in America. Chichén Itzá captured by Toltecs. Anasazi and Mississippian peoples emerge around this time.
		c. 1010 CE	*The Tale of Genji* written in Japan.
1024 CE	Conrad II becomes first king of Salian dynasty.		
1054 CE	Great Schism between eastern and western Christian churches.		

WESTERN ASIA, NORTHERN AFRICA, AND EUROPE		REST OF THE WORLD	
	1055 CE	Seljuk Turks oust Buyids.		
	1076 CE	Pope Gregory VII excommunicates emperor Henry IV; Henry goes to Canossa for forgiveness.		
	1084 CE	Henry IV invades Rome; ousts Gregory VII; installs Clement III as pope.		
	1085 CE	Pope Gregory VII dies in exile.		
	1106 CE	Henry IV dies; succeeded by Henry V.	c. 1100 CE	Islamic conquest of northern India marginalizes region's Buddhists. Zen Buddhism established in Japan. In Cambodia, work begins on Khmer temple of Angkor Wat. First Incas settle in Valley of Cuzco.
	1125 CE	Henry V dies childless; Salian dynasty ends.		
	1126 CE	Averroës born in Córdoba.		
			1192 CE	Minamoto Yoritomo becomes shogun (military ruler) of Japan.
c. 1200 CE			c. 1200 CE	Nomadic Mexica people settle on Lake Texcoco, a region dominated by Tepanecs; area later becomes heart of Aztec Empire. Anasazi complete major settlement, Pueblo Bonito.
			1215 CE	Genghis Khan captures Yenking (modern Beijing).
			1235 CE	Kingdom of Mali founded in western Africa.
	1258 CE	Mongol leader Hulagu Khan sacks Baghdad; end of Abbasid dynasty.		

GLOSSARY

Abbasids dynasty of caliphs formed by descendants of Mohammed's uncle Abbas; ruled from Baghdad (750–1258 CE) until it was sacked by Mongols. Accorded a purely religious function in Egypt, Abbasids held power there from 1261 to 1517 CE.

Achaemenids dynasty that ruled Persia between 550 and 330 BCE.

Ahura Mazda Zoroastrian god of light and truth.

Allah Arabic word for God.

Arabia desert peninsula lying to the east of the Mediterranean Sea.

Armenia region of the Transcaucasus between the Black Sea and the Caspian Sea.

Badr, Battle of battle near Medina in 624 CE that was Mohammed's first military victory. It damaged Meccan prestige, strengthened the political position of Muslims in Medina, and established Islam in Arabia.

Baghdad city built by Al-Mansur to appease the Persian Muslims; center of trade, industry, and Persian culture; destroyed by the Mongols.

Bayt al-Hikma (House of Wisdom) library and translation institute in Abbasid Baghdad.

Bedouin nomadic people of the Arabian Desert; converted to Islam around 622 CE; dominated non-Islamic population under the Umayyads; forced to yield power to the Abbasid dynasty around 750 CE.

Bosporus strait, 19 miles (30 km) long, that joins the Black Sea and the Sea of Marmara.

Buyids native dynasty that ruled in western Iran and Iraq in the period between the Arab and Turkish conquests (945–1055 CE).

caliph from *khalifah*, Arabic for "successor"; religious and political leader of Islam; successor to Mohammed. Competing caliphs divided the Islamic states.

caliphate office and realm held by a caliph.

Capetians ruling house of France from 987 to 1328 CE. The Capetians all descended from Robert the Strong (died 866 CE).

Cluny abbey near Mâcon, Burgundy, France, founded in 910 CE. The Cluniac movement that originated there strongly influenced the Roman Catholic Church, particularly monasticism, for the next 250 years.

Constantinople name for Byzantium (present-day Istanbul), which became the (Christian) residence of the emperor Constantine in 330 CE. In 395 CE, it became the capital of the eastern Roman Empire.

Ctesiphon capital of the ancient Persian Empire.

Damascus ancient city in Syria; residence of the Umayyad dynasty (661–750 CE); center of Arab culture and trade; famous for damask.

Euphrates river of western Asia that flows 1,740 miles (2,800 km) from eastern Turkey to the Persian Gulf.

Fatimids Shi'ite dynasty of caliphs in northern Africa (909–1171 CE); descended from Mohammed's daughter Fatima; conquered Egypt and founded Cairo around 969 CE.

Gnosticism philosophical and religious movement that was prominent in the Greco-Roman world in the second century CE. It had a profound influence on developing Christianity.

Golden Horn inlet of the Bosporus that forms a natural harbor at Constantinople (modern Istanbul).

Greek fire secret Byzantine weapon, used especially against Arabs at sieges of Constantinople in the seventh and eighth centuries CE. Its main constituent, naphtha (a highly combustible hydrocarbon), burned spontaneously when sprayed onto enemy ships.

Gur town founded by the Sassanian king Ardashir I to commemorate his victory over the Parthian king Artabanus; modern Firuzabad, Iran.

Hadith Arabic for "story"; companion book to the Koran; guide for Muslim daily life; details incidents in Mohammed's life and his maxims.

hegira Arabic for "flight"; journey of Mohammed from Mecca to Medina, September 20, 622 CE; used as the first date of the Muslim calendar; the starting point of Islam.

Hejaz region of Arabian Peninsula along the Red Sea coast.

Hephthalites nomadic people, originally from the Mongolian steppes, who created an empire in Persia and India in the sixth century CE.

Hormuz island in the Strait of Hormuz, between the Persian Gulf and the Gulf of Oman; site of battle in which Ardashir defeated the Parthians and killed Artabanus in 224 CE.

iconoclasm policy of destroying religious images (icons); introduced in the eighth century CE by the Byzantine emperor Leo III.

imam Arabic for "leader"; the head of the Muslim community.

Indus river of south Asia that flows 1,800 miles (2,900 km) from south-western Tibet to the Arabian Sea near modern Karachi (Pakistan).

Islam monotheistic religion worshipping Allah; founded by Mohammed in the seventh century CE. Its tenets, as revealed to Mohammed, are record-ed in the Koran.

jihad Arabic for "holy war"; Muslim duty to expand Allah's realm, to prop-agate Islam; led to the conquering of Mesopotamia, Syria, Egypt, northern Africa, central Asia, and Spain in the seventh and eighth centuries CE.

Kaaba Arabic for "cube"; stone cube in Mecca originally considered holy by most Arabs for its more than 300 statues. Mohammed considered it a religious relic of Allah built by Ishmael and condemned the polytheism. Although driven away in 622 CE, he returned to purge it in 629 CE, mak-ing it the central temple of Islam.

Karbala, Battle of battle in which the Umayyad military was victorious over the forces of the grandson of the prophet Mohammed. The battle secured the power of the Umayyad dynasty.

Koran scripture of Islam; regarded by the faithful as being revealed to Mohammed over 22 years and recorded by scribes; written in verses organized into 114 chapters, called *suras*; contains the history of Mohammed, references to the Bible, and principles of Islamic law.

Lombards central European Germanic people; conquered most of Italy in 568 CE, leaving Byzantine rule only on the coast and in the south. The Lombard Empire was subjected by Charlemagne in the eighth century CE.

Lotharingia kingdom belonging to Lothair (ruled 855–869 CE); dissolved after the king's death in 869 CE; modern Lorraine, France.

Maghreb region of northern Africa bordering the Mediterranean Sea and at one time also comprising Spain.

Magyars Finno-Ugric people who began occupying the middle basin of the Danube River in the ninth century CE; ancestors of modern Hungarians.

Manichaeism religion founded by Mani in Mesopotamia; combines elements of Christianity, Zoroastrianism, Buddhism, and others; postulates two competing principles of good (referred to as light, God, the human soul) and evil (as seen in darkness, the devil, the human body). Mani considered knowledge of light through his teachings and an ascetic way of life as the way to salvation. The Manichaeans were persecuted by Persian kings and Roman emperors.

Medina Arabian oasis town to which Mohammed fled in 622 CE; originally named Yathrib; renamed Madinat al-Nabi (the city of the prophet), or Medina. Mohammed converted its already largely monotheistic Jewish population, becoming its theocratic leader. Medina waged war against Mecca until 628 CE.

Merovingians Frankish dynasty (481–751 CE) that ruled an area of Europe roughly corresponding to modern France. Its rulers are regarded as the earliest French kings.

Mesopotamia area in western Asia surrounding the Euphrates and Tigris rivers. (The word comes from the Greek meaning "between two rivers.") Floods and irrigation made the land fertile, and around 4500 BCE, the first agricultural settlements were founded there.

Monophysitism fifth-century-CE doctrine—from the Greek *monos* (single) and *physis* (nature)—that con-tended that Jesus Christ had only a single nature, which was divine, not human. That idea conflicted with the orthodox doctrine that Christ was at once human and divine.

Muslims worshippers of Allah; members of Islam.

Nestorianism doctrine of Nestorius (c. 382–451 CE), patriarch of Constantinople (428–431 CE). He postulated that Jesus Christ acted as a single person but did not have conjoined divine and human natures, being purely human on earth and purely god in heaven. In consequence, he contended that Mary could not be called Mother of God; she begot the man Jesus, while God begot his divine aspect. This doctrine gained followers, notably in the New Persian Empire, against the orthodox Christian belief that Christ has two distinct natures, divine and human, joined in both person and substance. In the fifth century CE, Nestorianism spread throughout the Byzantine Empire but was declared heretical by the Council of Ephesus (431 CE). The Nestorians became powerful in Persia, India, China, and Mongolia in early medieval times.

New Persian Empire ruled by the Sassanid dynasty; founded by Ardashir in 224 CE; conquered by Arabs in 651 CE; notable for coexistence of many religions, including Christianity, Nestorianism, and Manichaeism.

Ostia ancient town at the mouth of the Tiber River; port of Rome.

Parni nomadic tribe living to the east of the Caspian Sea. Its members founded the Parthian Empire.

Parthia kingdom founded around 240 BCE; part of present-day Afghanistan and Iran.

Parthians inhabitants of Parthia; acclaimed for their equestrian skills; regularly waged war with the Roman Empire; conquered by rebelling Persians, who founded the New Persian Kingdom (224 CE).

Persis ancient country in western Asia (present-day southwestern Iran). Its name derives from that of the Parsua, a nomadic people who settled there in the seventh century BCE.

Petra ancient city of western Asia in present-day Jordan; center of an Arab kingdom in Hellenistic and Roman times.

Punjab region of northwestern India. Its name derives from Persian words meaning "five rivers."

Reconquista Spanish for "reconquest"; Christian reconquering of occupied Spain from the Muslims (11th–13th centuries CE).

Roncesvalles village in Navarre (northern Spain) near which the Basques massacred the rearguard of Charlemagne's army in 778 CE.

Samarra town on the Tigris River that became the capital of the Abbasid caliphate in 836 CE.

Sassanids dynasty of kings (224–651 CE); captured Mesopotamia and eastern Syria from the Byzantines in the fourth century CE; conquered Jerusalem in 614 CE; defeated by Alexius in 628 CE.

Saxons ancient people of northern Germany; conquered parts of England in the fifth and sixth centuries CE.

Seljuks Turks who captured Baghdad from the Shi'ites; established power in Persia around 1055 CE; conquered Anatolia in 1071 CE. Their kingdom had disintegrated by the end of the 12th century CE.

Shi'ites supporters of Mohammed's son-in-law Ali; seceded from orthodox Islam after the murder of Hussein in 680 CE. Shi'ites (from *shi'ah*, Arabic for "partisan") believe that their leaders (imams) are divinely guided and have the right to Muslim leadership.

Silk Road ancient overland trade route that extended for 4,000 miles (6,400 km) and linked China and the West. First used as a caravan route, the road ran from Xi'an, China, along the Great Wall, through the Pamir Mountains, into Afghanistan, and on to the eastern Mediterranean Sea, where goods were taken onward by boat, mainly to Rome and Venice. On westbound journeys, the principal cargo was silk; wool, gold, and silver were the main commodities carried in the opposite direction.

Sunnis orthodox Muslims who follow the Sunna (the body of Islamic custom).

Tigris river of western Asia that flows 1,180 miles (1,900 km) from eastern Turkey to the Persian Gulf.

Umayyads dynasty of caliphs in Damascus from the Umayyad clan that dominated the Arab world, including non-Islamic population (c. 661–750 CE); ousted by the Abbasids.

Vikings Scandinavian seafaring warriors who raided and colonized wide areas of Europe from the 9th century to the 11th century CE. Some of them settled in northern France, where they became Normans.

Yarmuk tributary of the Jordan River in western Asia; site of a decisive battle in which Khalid ibn al-Walid defeated Byzantine forces in 636 CE.

Zoroastrianism traditional religion of Persians prior to conversion to Islam; founded by Zoroaster; posited competing spirits of good and evil.

MAJOR HISTORICAL FIGURES

Abu Bakr (c. 573–634 CE) first leader of Islam after the death of the prophet Mohammed in 632 CE; began jihad, seizing Syrian territory from the Persians.

Ardashir I king of Persia from 224 to 241 CE.

Artabanus V king of Parthia from 213 to 224 CE.

Averroës (1126–1198 CE) also known as Ibn Ruhd; Córdoba-born Muslim writer on religious law, philosophy, and medicine.

Avicenna (980–1037 CE) also known as Ibn Sina; born in Bukhara; author of the encyclopedic works *Kitab ash-shifa* (Book of Healing) and *Al-Qanan fi at-tibb* (The Canon of Medicine).

Charlemagne Frankish king from 768 to 814 CE; founded the Holy Roman Empire, of which he was emperor from 800 CE.

Charles Martel ruler of Austrasia (modern northeastern France and southwestern Germany) between 714 and 741 CE; fought against Alemanni, Bavarians, and Saxons; defeated an Islamic army near Poitiers in 732 CE.

Clovis I king of the Franks between 481 and 511 CE; conquered most of Gaul; defeated Alemanni and Visigoths; converted in 496 CE.

Cnut (died 1035 CE) Danish king who united Denmark, England, and Norway into a single kingdom; also known as Canute.

Constantine the Great Roman emperor between 306 and 337 CE; ruled initially in the west only but became absolute sovereign in 324 CE; built Constantinople; legalized Christianity.

Firdawsi Persian poet who wrote *Shah-nama* (Book of Kings) around 1010 CE.

Genghis Khan (c. 1162–1227 CE) first leader to unite the Mongols, whom he led on a campaign of conquest that took in China and some Islamic empires.

Harun al-Rashid caliph who brought the Abbasid dynasty to the peak of its power; ruled between 786 and 809 CE.

Heraclius Byzantine emperor between 610 and 641 CE; began counteroffensive against Khosrow II in 622 CE; weakened the Persian Empire by his victories in the center of the realm in 627 CE.

Hugh Capet king of France between 987 and 996 CE; gradually unified the previously fragmented country. The Capetian dynasty that he founded endured until 1328 CE.

Julian the Apostate Roman emperor who ruled between 361 and 363 CE; limited the rights of Christians.

Khosrow I king of Persia between 531 and 579 CE.

Khosrow II king of Persia between 590 and 628 CE; seized Syria and Jerusalem from the Byzantines; defeated by Heraclius in 627 CE.

Leo III Byzantine emperor between 717 and 741 CE; sometimes known as Leo the Isaurian; gained the throne after several succession conflicts; withstood an Arab siege; made the Byzantine Empire a buffer against Islamic expansion.

Mani (c. 216–276 CE) Persian prophet who founded Manichaeism.

Mansur, Al- caliph of the Abbasid dynasty from 754 to 775 CE; founder of Baghdad; attempted to unify the realm through religion.

Marcus Aurelius emperor of Rome between 161 and 180 CE.

Mu'awiyah first Umayyad caliph; ruled between 661 and 680 CE; moved the capital of Islam from Medina to Damascus; opposed Ali and his followers; dominated Syria and Egypt. After Ali's death, he bought off Ali's son Hassan to become absolute sovereign of the Arabian Empire.

Othman ibn Affan third caliph; ruled between 644 and 656 CE; son-in-law of the prophet Mohammed; founder of the Umayyad dynasty.

Shapur I king of Persia between 241 and 272 CE; expanded the New Persian Empire to the Himalayas; conquered Armenia; defeated the Byzantines in Antioch, taking many Syrian prisoners of war. Christianity spread throughout his realm.

Shapur II king of Persia between 309 and 379 CE; captured parts of eastern Syria and Mesopotamia from the eastern Roman Empire; defeated Julian in 363 CE; brought the New Persian Empire to its apex.

Yazdegerd III last Sassanid king of Persia; ruled between 632 and 651 CE.

Yazid I caliph between 680 and 683 CE; son and successor of Mu'awiyah.

RESOURCES FOR FURTHER STUDY

BOOKS

Allen, Lindsay. *The Persian Empire*. Chicago, IL, 2005.

Barbero, Alessandro (translated by Allan Cameron). *Charlemagne: Father of a Continent*. Berkeley, CA, 2004.

Besancon, Alain (translated by Jane Marie Todd). *The Forbidden Image: An Intellectual History of Iconoclasm*. Chicago, IL, 2000.

Bowersock, G.W. *Julian the Apostate*. Cambridge, MA, 1978.

Burgess, Glyn (trans. and ed.). *Chanson de Roland*. New York, 1990.

Christie, Neil. *The Lombards: The Ancient Longobards*. Cambridge, MA, 1995.

Cleary, Thomas. *The Wisdom of the Prophet: Sayings of Muhammad*. Boston, MA, 2001.

Clot, André (translated by John Howe). *Harun al-Rashid and the World of the Thousand and One Nights*. New York, 1989.

Cowdrey, H.E.J. *Pope Gregory VII, 1073–1085*. New York, 1998.

Crouch, David. *The Normans: The History of a Dynasty*. London, England, 2002.

Curtis, Vesta Sarkhosh, and Sarah Stewart (eds.). *Birth of the Persian Empire*. New York, 2005.

Dakake, Maria Massi. *The Charismatic Community: Shi'ite Identity in Early Islam*. Albany, NY, 2007.

Dawood, N.J. (trans.). *The Koran*. New York, 1990.

Duby, Georges (translated by Juliet Vale). *France in the Middle Ages, 987–1460: From Hugh Capet to Joan of Arc*. Cambridge, MA, 1991.

Dunbabin, Jean. *France in the Making, 843–1180*. New York, 2000.

El-Hibri, Tayeb. *Reinterpreting Islamic Historiography: Harun al-Rashid and the Narrative of the Abbasid Caliphate*. New York, 1999.

Fakhry, Majid. *Averroes, Aquinas, and the Rediscovery of Aristotle in Western Europe*. Washington, DC, 1997.

Geary, Patrick J. *Before France and Germany: The Creation and Transformation of the Merovingian World*. New York, 1988.

Goodman, Lenn Evan. *Avicenna*. Ithaca, NY, 2006.

Hall, R.A. *The World of the Vikings*. New York, 2007.

Hallam, Elizabeth M., and Judith Everard. *Capetian France, 987–1328*. New York, 2001.

Hawting, G.R. *The First Dynasty of Islam: The Umayyad Caliphate, AD 661–750*. New York, 2000.

Heer, Friedrich (translated by Janet Sondheimer). *The Holy Roman Empire*. New York, 1968.

Hoeller, Stephan A. *Gnosticism: New Light on the Ancient Tradition of Inner Knowing*. Wheaton, IL, 2002.

Kaegi, Walter Emil. *Heraclius, Emperor of Byzantium*. New York, 2003.

Lawrence, C.H. *Medieval Monasticism*. New York, 2001.

Le Strange, G. *Baghdad during the Abbasid Caliphate: From Contemporary Arabic and Persian Sources*. New York, 1972.

Losleben, Elizabeth. *The Bedouin of the Middle East*. Minneapolis, MN, 2003.

Mayor, Adrienne. *Greek Fire, Poison Arrows, and Scorpion Bombs: Biological and Chemical Warfare in the Ancient World*. Woodstock, NY, 2003.

McCaughrean, Geraldine (ed.). *One Thousand and One Arabian Nights*. New York, 1999.

Morgan, David. *The Mongols*. New York, 1986.

Mullins, Edwin B. *Cluny: In Search of God's Lost Empire*. New York, 2006.

Nicolle, David. *Yarmuk, AD 636: The Muslim Conquest of Syria*. Westport, CT, 2005.

Nomachi, Kazuyoshi. *Mecca the Blessed, Medina the Radiant: The Holiest Cities of Islam*. New York, 1997.

O'Callaghan, Joseph F. *Reconquest and Crusade in Medieval Spain*. Philadelphia, PA, 2003.

Payaslian, Simon. *The History of Armenia*. New York, 2007.

Pollard, Justin. *Alfred the Great: The Man Who Made England*. London, England, 2005.

Posnov, Mikhail (translated by Thomas E. Herman). *The History of the Christian Church until the Great Schism of 1054*. Bloomington, IN, 2004.

Roesdahl, Else (translated by Susan M. Margeson and Kirsten Williams). *The Vikings*. New York, 1998.

Safran, Janina M. *The Second Umayyad Caliphate: The Articulation of Caliphal Legitimacy in al-Andalus*. Cambridge, MA, 2000.

Sherwani, Muhammad Habibur Rahman Khan (translated by Syed Moinul Haq). *Hazrat Abu Bakr: The First Caliph of Islam*. Lahore, Pakistan, 1963.

Smith, Richard L. *Ahmad al-Mansur: Islamic Visionary*. New York, 2006.

Smoley, Richard. *Forbidden Faith: The Gnostic Legacy from the Gospels to the Da Vinci Code*. San Francisco, CA, 2006.

Stephenson, Carl. *Mediaeval Feudalism*. Ithaca, NY, 1942.

Swarup, Ram. *Understanding the Hadith: The Sacred Traditions of Islam*. Amherst, NY, 2002.

Sypeck, Jeff. *Becoming Charlemagne: Europe, Baghdad, and the Empires of AD 800*. New York, 2006.

———. *The Holy Roman Empire and Charlemagne in World History*. Berkeley Heights, NJ, 2002.

Thubron, Colin. *Shadow of the Silk Road*. New York, 2007.

Ullmann, Walter. *The Carolingian Renaissance and the Idea of Kingship*. London, England, 1969.

Weinfurter, Stefan (translated by Barbara M. Bowlus). *The Salian Century: Main Currents in an Age of Transition*. Philadelphia, PA, 1999.

White, Carolinne (ed.). *Early Christian Lives: Life of Antony by Athanasius, Life of Paul of Thebes by Jerome, Life of Hilarion by Jerome, Life of Malchus by Jerome, Life of Martin of Tours by Sulpicius Severus, Life of Benedict by Gregory the Great*. New York, 1998.

Wood, Frances. *The Silk Road: Two Thousand Years in the Heart of Asia*. Berkeley, CA, 2002.

WEB SITES

Abbasids
Article about the family that formed the last Arab caliphates; includes dates for the various caliphs
http://i-cias.com/e.o/abbasids.htm

Abu Bakr
Brief account of the life and work of the prophet Mohammed's close adviser
http://www.hyperhistory.com/online_n2/people_n2/ppersons4_n2/abu.html

Ahura Mazda
Article on the Zoroastrian god of light and truth; includes links to several topics of related interest.
http://www.livius.org/ag-ai/ahuramazda/ahuramazda.html

Alfred the Great
Outline of the king's reign; includes links to his writings and accounts of the lives of other English monarchs
http://www.royalinsight.gov.uk/output/Page25.asp

Averroës
Biography of the influential Islamic religious philosopher; includes extensive links to other resources
http://www.muslimphilosophy.com/ir

Bedouin
Web site that covers all aspects of the culture and history of the desert-dwelling people
http://www.geographia.com/egypt/sinai/bedouin.htm

Benedict of Nursia
Comprehensive biographical Web site; includes links to further articles and images
http://saints.sqpn.com/saintb02.htm

Chanson de Roland
Original French text of the 11th-century-CE poem; includes an English translation by Charles Scott Moncrief and commentary
http://www.orbilat.com/Languages/French/Texts/Period_02/1090-La_Chanson_de_Roland.htm

Charlemagne
Extensive biography of the Frankish leader who united much of western Europe under his rule
http://www.historyworld.net/wrldhis/PlainTextHistories.asp?historyid=aa20

Einhard: The Life of Charlemagne
Online English-language edition of the classic
biography of Charlemagne, translated by Samuel Epes
Turner
http://www.fordham.edu/halsall/basis/einhard.html

Gnosticism
Comprehensive introduction to the structure and
significance of the religious movement and its world
view
http://www.webcom.com/gnosis/gnintro.htm

Great Schism
Detailed account of the causes and consequences of the
rift between the eastern and western Christian churches
in 1054 CE
http://mb-soft.com/believe/txc/gschism.htm

Heraclius
Biography of the Roman emperor; includes suggestions for
further reading
http://www.roman-emperors.org/heraclis.htm

Islam
Web site that provides a comprehensive outline of Muslim
beliefs as well as an account of the religion's historical
development
http://www.bbc.co.uk/religion/religions/islam

Julian the Apostate
Account of the life and historical significance of the
Roman emperor who rejected Christianity and reverted
to pagan ways
http://www.roman-empire.net/collapse/julian.html

Lombards
Brief description of the people's origins and achievements
http://www.hyw.com/books/history/Langobar.htm

Mecca
Description of the city; includes a list of key dates in the
history of the city
http://i-cias.com/e.o/mecca.htm

Merovingians
Introduction to the Frankish royal line; includes a dynastic
family tree
http://www.ordotempli.org/the_merovingians.htm

One Thousand and One Nights
Web site that contextualizes the Arabic story collection and
provides a link to the famous English translation of the
work by Richard Burton
http://www.al-bab.com/arab/literature/nights.htm

Persian Empire
Detailed description of the civilization; includes useful maps
and time lines
http://www.crystalinks.com/persia.html

Silk Road
Story of one of the world's most historically important
trade routes and its influences on the cultures of China,
central Asia, and Europe
http://www.ess.uci.edu/~oliver/silk.html

Sunni and Shi'ite Muslims
Essay explaining the origin of the central split in the
Muslim world
http://hnn.us/articles/934.html

Umayyads
Short account of the first Muslim dynasty; includes
suggestions for further reading
http://www.princeton.edu/~batke/itl/denise/umayyads.htm

INDEX